DIGITAL CORPORATE CITIZENSHIP

THE BUSINESS RESPONSE TO THE DIGITAL DIVIDE

Craig Warren Smith

The Center on Philanthropy at Indiana University

Digital Corporate Citizenship
Published by The Center on Philanthropy
at Indiana University

©2002 Craig Warren Smith

For information, contact:
The Center on Philanthropy at Indiana University
550 W. North St., Suite 301
Indianapolis, IN 46202-3272
317-274-4200
www.philanthropy.iupui.edu

Library of Congress Cataloging-in-Publication Data

Smith, Craig Warren.
   Digital corporate citizenship: the business response to the digital
divide / Craig Warren Smith.
      p. cm.
Includes bibliographical references and index.
   ISBN 1-884354-20-3 (alk. paper)
   1. Digital divide. 2. Information technology–Social aspects.
3. Social responsibility of business. 4. Corporations—Charitable
contributions. I. Title.
   HN49.156 S65 2002

                              2002003737

Design and layout by Beyond Words, Inc.

To Ali and Shelley,
who offered unconditional support.

About the Author

Craig Warren Smith holds a joint appointment at Harvard University's Center for International Development and MIT Media Lab and is an internationally recognized authority on corporate citizenship and philanthropy. Former director of the Digital Partnership Program of the Conference Board of New York, he has assumed many roles in the global movement to close the digital divide. He assisted Microsoft in crafting its policies concerning the support of nonprofit organizations. As a senior consultant to the United Nations, he helped establish the framework for UN Secretary-General Kofi Annan's Task Force on Information Technology. He also founded several nongovernmental organizations focused on this issue, including Digital Partners and DigitalDivide.org. His work on the digital divide has been supported by the Ford Foundation, Rockefeller Foundation, W.K. Kellogg Foundation, Open Society Institute, and others.

Contents

Foreword

The 21st century is sure to bring new and argumentative discussion about the role that business is to play in addressing the division in access to technological developments — the so-called digital divide. Craig Smith has provided in this volume a report of extensive interviews with corporate executives and research on companies at the forefront of technology and its use in society today.

These findings make a significant contribution to our understanding of the impact corporations can have when they turn their resources to addressing an important societal need. The importance of integrating doing good for society with doing well for business is clearly articulated. Understanding how corporate citizenship needs to be an integrated activity within various business functions (marketing, government relations, research, human resources and management) has been the focus of much of the literature on business and society for the past decade. Craig Smith has provided us with important insights into this field over the years. His seminal article in the *Harvard Business Review* in May/June 1994, "The New Corporate Philanthropy," provides a preface for this work.

This book will be confirmed as another seminal work by the end of this decade. It is a privilege for the Center on Philanthropy at Indiana University to be a partner with Mr. Smith in sharing this work with a larger audience. Practitioners and scholars of business alike will find important insights to be utilized in their work as they address the digital divide.

Dwight Burlingame
March, 2002

Preface

The leading international computer, telecom, and media corporations are facing a quandary.

On the one hand, the downturn in markets has forced them to reserve their attention for their most affluent customers in the most advanced markets. On the other hand, all these companies understand that their long-term fortunes lie not in the wealthy few but in billions of less-affluent citizens who will soon be connected to computer networks.

How can these companies conceivably remake themselves to be relevant to the poor at a time when market conditions force them to be extremely short-term oriented and risk averse?

This conundrum puts this book into perspective. It describes how shrewd middle managers in 60 of the largest digital corporations have tried to do the impossible: Formulate big attention-grabbing technology initiatives with big social impacts–and do so with the least possible outlay of funds and without causing their companies' employees to divert their attention from their top customers.

Don't let the term "corporate citizenship" in the title confuse you. This book is about hard-nosed business strategy. The idea is to create projects that seem philanthropic, but that serve as a real tool for competitive success, helping internal managers build valuable business relationships. It is about reaching out to under-served groups in the United States, such as African-American and Hispanic populations. It is also about winning over skeptical government bureaucrats in places like China, Brazil, and Mexico where the digital economy is just beginning to heat up.

Part of the problem is that most governments do not have a clue about how to encourage companies to formulate such social initiatives. In the United States, Europe, and most of the developing countries, regulators have done little to reward companies that creatively respond to the digital divide–the gap between those able to benefit from digital technology and those who can't–or punish those that do not. For their part, universities and non-governmental organizations (NGOs) are also to blame. Though they form partnerships with the big multinational companies to showcase beneficial uses of this or that technology, they do little to help these same companies understand how to gain a business advantage in the process of closing the digital divide.

This book is not just for corporate managers seeking best practices as digital corporate citizens. It is also for reformers in governments, NGOs, and academia. They may find in the following pages ideas about how to use the carrots and sticks available to them to coax companies to be creative in finding out-of-the-box business models that serve the needs of the poor.

Craig Warren Smith
Cambridge, Massachusetts, 2002

Acknowledgments

M any thanks to Melissa Berman of the Conference Board for providing a platform for conducting the initial research; to Dwight Burlingame and Lois Sherman for persevering during the writing and editing process; to Susan Berresford, Michele Kahane and John Weiser at the Ford Foundation for helping to inspire the project; to Joan Shigekawa of the Rockefeller Foundation for encouraging me to extend the framework internationally; to Geoffrey Kirkman, Sandy Pentland, and Colin McClay for providing a base at Harvard and MIT to complete this work; to Steven Zeilke of Motorola, for many hours of thought-provoking discussion; to Gale McClure of the Kellogg Foundation for crucial financial support; to Justin Thumler of Digital Partners for encouragement in the early phase.

Executive Summary

Between 1997 and 2001, when the digital revolution had captured the public's imagination, a number of high-tech corporations mostly located in the United States created a new class of social projects. They are larger and more ambitious than any previously attempted by the corporate sector. Valued at up to hundreds of millions of dollars each, they are called "signature initiatives" by insiders. Many have been remarkably sustainable, even after the dot-com crash of 2001 and the layoff of thousands of employees in the companies that sponsored them.

Do these initiatives represent a departure from the lean-and-mean corporate culture of Silicon Valley? Or are they somehow aligned with the business strategies emerging from the new economy? Given the public's growing appreciation of the importance of harnessing digital technology to achieve social change, an examination of this new wave of corporate citizenship practices has special implications for society at large, as well as for companies themselves, which are seeking new out-of-the-box pathways in competitive success. This study, based on interviews with 60 leading computer, telecommunications, and media corporations, looks beyond the companies' descriptions of social programs on web sites and in annual reports to explore why they have created these initiatives, how the initiatives fit into corporate management structures, and what they say about the role that nonprofit corporations can play in today's new-economy corporations.

Crucial to the analysis is the notion that signature initiatives are not shaped top-down by the personal involvement of CEOs, as has often been the case in corporate philanthropy projects of

1

the past. Nor have they emerged bottom-up from the ranks of employees. Rather, most surfaced from the companies' mid-ranks. Almost all are formed by middle managers from a spectrum of internal departments that, for quite different reasons, have learned how nonprofit organizations can contribute to their business strategies. The starring role in these internal alliances is not always played by "community affairs" departments, where relations with nonprofit organizations are traditionally housed. In some cases, the lead role is played by human resources departments, government affairs departments, marketing units, or even by research and development divisions. All five of these internal units (or "business functions" as middle-managers call them) are much closer to the companies' core businesses than to typical corporate philanthropy. In recent years, each of these internal functions has broadened and deepened its ties with nonprofit organizations. Indeed, it appears that nonprofits are more broadly represented in the management structures of new-economy companies than in old-economy companies, where they are more commonly housed in the companies' in-house foundations. Gradually, high-tech companies are learning to deploy their technology and management systems to transform their ties with nonprofits into powerful social initiatives and to do so with very minimal additional cash outlay.

These new expressions of "digital corporate citizenship" represent an important dimension in the global movement to close the digital divide and, as such, contribute to an understanding of how social problems can be resolved in the digital era. But these initiatives also have implications for corporate strategy and, some say, they hold a key to the brand image of Internet corporations that are eager to be perceived as positive assets for society. What may emerge from these in-house initiatives is a new way of doing business–a "soft path" to the pursuit of business success for these companies. This soft approach aims to complement, not replace, the hardball tactics normally practiced in their core business operations. However, not all companies have the management know-how or the leadership to shape and sustain signature initiatives that can serve business purposes. Some initiatives, once created, are hobbled by widespread misunderstanding of their nature by nonprofit leaders and by the companies' own employees.

If the social initiatives of high-tech corporations are able to find a strong and enduring place in the core strategies of high-tech businesses, it will be a sign that these companies have the flexibility and leadership needed to reinvent themselves for relevance in a global, networked world. If not, government officials and activists wanting to reign in the power of high-tech giants may well gain the leverage they need to force these companies to reform their business practices.

CHAPTER ONE

A Social Movement Arises Among High-Tech Giants

With dot-coms crashing around her, Hewlett-Packard (H-P) Chief Executive Carly Fiorina stepped up to a podium in late 2000 and made an announcement that shocked the *digerati:* H-P would commit $1 billion "on behalf of itself and its partners" to apply its technology to create wealth and empowerment for the world's poorest citizens. Beta tests for this effort would be conducted soon in 1,000 of the world's most impoverished villages. H-P declared itself ready to find partners in a historic effort to spread wealth "at the bottom of the pyramid."[1]

Huh? One billion dollars? For the poorest of the poor? It seemed like an odd time to announce what appeared to many to be the most significant antipoverty effort in corporate history.[2] The NASDAQ was in free-fall. Smug Wall Street analysts wondered whether this photogenic lady CEO had what it takes to remake stodgy H-P into a lean dot-com survivor.

The business media were dazzled. *Fortune* lauded it as an antipoverty breakthrough, calling it "the most visionary step ever taken by an IT company." But the media attention led to high expectations and, ultimately, to the dismay of nonprofit organizations that had traditionally come to the venerable

---

[1] The term "bottom of the pyramid" refers to a concept of management experts C. K. Prahahad and Stewart Hart in a widely distributed (but as of 2002, still unpublished) article, "Strategies for the Bottom of the Pyramid," in which the authors introduced the idea that sustainable business success can be found only among the lowest-income four billion consumers "at the bottom of the pyramid" and that information technology makes possible business models that can greatly reduce costs and enhance the productivity of the poor. See www.digitaldividend.org.

[2] By 2002, Ms. Fiorini was locked in a bitter internal dispute over her efforts to acquire COMPAQ Computers. In this atmosphere, H-P discreetly announced a scaling back of the initiative.

company for support. Proposals flooded Hewlett-Packard's Palo Alto headquarters from grantseekers wanting to be appointed as H-P's partners in this historic effort. But they learned that the company's high-minded effort to achieve breakthroughs in the elimination of world poverty had very little to do with philanthropic support of the sort that grantseekers are accustomed to solicit. "We had to drive home the point that this initiative is not about philanthropy at all but a fundamental new way of doing business at H-P," said Robert Granger, one of the H-P managers who had given birth to the effort.[3]

What was going on? The question pertains not just to H-P's project, which was called "World e-Inclusion" and which many consider to be before its time, but to a whole class of corporate social initiatives.

That question is at the heart of this report. Its investigation covers not just Hewlett-Packard's and Ms. Fiorini's bold initiative (now called "e-Inclusion Solutions)[4] but 60 other large high-tech companies, many of which have created social initiatives of a similar scale and potential impact. What these initiatives have in common is that they all hope to demonstrate the social value of their latest information technologies. And they are all conceived in ways that depart from conventional business practices–and from conventional corporate philanthropy as well. This report is not meant as a systematic chronicling of these efforts, but it inquires into their meaning–as perceived by strategists within the companies themselves and by nonprofit leaders who have formed close ties with these companies. Furthermore, the report looks beyond the list of flagship social initiatives to examine the underlying pattern of corporate/nonprofit relationships in these companies.

The Study

The seeds of this investigation were planted in 1995-96 at Microsoft, where I was a consultant. My assignment was to establish a policy framework for the company's ties to nonprofit

---

[3] Interview in Vancouver, WA, 2000.
[4] For an update on the e-Inclusion initiative of Hewlett-Packard, which was renamed e-Inclusion Solutions in late 2001, see www.hp.com/hpinfo/community.

organizations. Occurring at a time when Microsoft was already attracting government scrutiny for its dominance in computer software, the consultancy involved examining how the company's policies could eventually put it on a collision course with society's guardians. In this consultancy, I learned of the need for high-tech companies to respond to those focused on the digital divide.[5] In the mid-1990s, that term was used mostly by social activists and researchers who cited empirical evidence that the personal computer revolution was driving a wedge between those able to benefit from digital technology and those who were not.[6] Later, in 1998, that Microsoft experience led to another consultancy, with the Ford Foundation, in which the assignment was to strengthen the foundation's ties with corporations. In a discussion at Ford Foundation headquarters, the foundation's president, Susan Berresford,[7] was in a highly reflective mood. She wondered whether the Ford Foundation, and the governments and nonprofit networks the foundation works with, could or *should* relate directly to the corporate giants whose digital strategies seemed destined to impose big changes in society just as they have in the economy. Could the Ford Foundation make more of a difference, she pondered, if it were to form partnerships with high-tech corporations in ways similar to the business-to-business alliances that are common among those companies? By forming common cause with them, would there be a way to affect their practices? She knew that few of her colleagues in philanthropy's leadership ranks had direct ties to the new titans of digital industries. "Do these corporations have the incentives to be drawn into partnerships on behalf of the social issues we care about?" she wondered.

---

[5] The term *digital divide* as used here refers to the gap between those able to benefit from digital technology and those who can't. For a typology of initiatives that seek to define and resolve the Digital Divide, see http://philanthropy.com/free/resources/technology/digitaldivide.htm. Also see www.DigitalDivide.org.

[6] For a compilation of domestic US statistics and resources on the digital divide, see David Bolt and Ray Crawford, *Digital Divide*, TV Books, LLC, 2000. For global perspectives, the best compilation of data on the *problematique* of the digital divide can be found in the annual reports of the United Nations Development Programme. See especially *Human Development Report, 2001*, New York, Oxford University Press, 2001.

[7] Ford Foundation offices, January 13, 1998.

This discussion triggered a process of research that led to this report. Because high-tech corporations are interested parties, they were not asked to be its sponsors. The initial research grant came from the Ford Foundation itself, and soon other foundations joined in as more layers were built onto the original study. Funds for the research contained herein were also provided by the Rockefeller Foundation, Open Society Institute, Markle Foundation, Kellogg Foundation, and the Charles Stewart Mott Foundation.[8]

At first, interviews were conducted in the United States and focused on corporate strategies unique to companies' North American operations. But they were eventually extended to overseas locations of U.S. corporations. Finally, in 2000, the research was extended to a few corporations based outside the United States, as the author took on yet another consulting assignment. This time, the task was to support United Nations Secretary-General Kofi Annan, who sought assistance in formulating the framework for a United Nations Task Force on Information and Communications Technology.

The bulk of the analysis presented in the following pages resulted from interviews conducted with executives in three industries–computers, telecommunications, and media. At the time, the companies involved were embarked on a seemingly nonstop process of imploding, merging, and restructuring, which led to an unprecedented concentration of communications power in the hands of a few dominant corporations.[9] Their fortunes rose and fell with dramatic intensity. Only the very largest companies, the ones that were thought to be able to shape markets as well as gain market share, were sought out for interviews.

Why these companies? There is no widespread agreement about whether these companies are prime-movers of

---

[8] Several of these foundations, including Markle, Rockefeller, Open Society Institute, and Mott, were supporters of "Seeking Solutions to the *Digital Divide*," co-organized by this author, which included background papers that extended the research originally commissioned by the Ford Foundation. The Kellogg Foundation's support was earmarked to the development of Digital Partners Institute, which continued the research.

[9] An indictment of the media convergence appeared in a series of articles in *The Nation* magazine in 1999. See "The New Global Media," http://past.thenation.com/issue/99129.

technological innovation, or whether that role is fulfilled by smaller, more nimble, companies.[10] However, in the realm of corporate citizenship, it is clear that the largest companies were innovators in *management*.[11] Just as these companies were introducing decentralized management structures and just-in-time inventory management, it seemed logical that they also might be introducing changes in corporate citizenship[12] practices. Furthermore, these companies were able to command investments in research and business development that could actually create markets. Clearly, the social initiatives of these corporations had important implications for society at large.

The research began in 1998 with the convening of small groups of executives in informal discussion, about 20 participants per gathering. The meetings took place in New York City (1998, hosted by The Conference Board), San Francisco (1999, hosted by California Cable Television Associations), and Seattle (1999, hosted by a trendy dot-com, Real Networks). Smaller meetings were held in Boston (2000, co-hosted by Harvard University's Center for International Development and MIT Media Lab), Hong Kong (2001, hosted by Pacific Century CyberWorks) and Banglore (2001, hosted by InfoSys).

Following these sessions, the author conducted one-on-one interviews at corporate headquarters with the executives and managers who appeared responsible for their companies' policies on social initiatives. The list included corporate chief executives who were particularly active in the movement to close the digital divide, such as 3Com's Eric Benhamou; executives who oversee "external relations" of companies, such as AOL Time Warner's George Vradenburg; those who direct "government relations,"

---

[10] *New Rules for the New Economy*, Kevin Kelly, Viking, 1998; *The Fourth Wave: Business in the 20th Century*, Herman Bryant Maynard, Jr., Susan Mehrtens, Berrett-Kohler Publishers, Inc., 1993; and *The Friction-Free Economy*, T.G. Lewis, HarperCollins, 1997.

[11] See *Harvard Business Review on Managing High-Tech Industries*, Harvard Business School Press, 1999. This is a collection of articles in the HBR journal that have defined the pattern of management innovation being introduced by high-tech companies.

[12] The term *corporate citizenship* as used here refers to the sum total of all the companies' efforts to support social goals through business practices–ranging from establishing ethical codes of conduct to proactive efforts to right society's ills. For a perspective on corporate citizenship as a field, see "The Promotion of Corporate Citizenship," by Craig Smith, Indiana University Center on Philanthropy, *Essays on Philanthropy*, No. 26.

such as Microsoft's Brad Smith; those who oversee overall strategy for their companies, such as Christine Hemrick of Cisco Systems; those who set policy for their company's philanthropy, such as WorldCom's Diane Strahn; and finally, those who manage policy areas related to philanthropy, such as marketing, human resources, government relations, research, and public relations, including heads of foreign subsidiaries.

In the early phases of the study, executives were hard to pin down even for telephone interviews. But as public attention to the digital divide issue rose to a fever pitch, the companies were more willing to talk, and some generously created day-long sessions in which managers of various ranks, units, and divisions were queried. The list came to include 60 companies, which together comprise approximately a 70 percent global market share in information technology fields. Despite its scope, the report clearly focuses on North America-based transnational corporations.

The Companies

The companies interviewed include AOL Time Warner, Acer, Adobe, amazon.com, Apple, Ameritech (later acquired by SBC Communications), AT&T, Bay Networks, Bell Atlantic, Bell South, Bertelsmann, Computer Associates, Cisco Systems, Compaq (possibly merging with Hewlett-Packard as of late 2001), Critical Path, Dell, Disney, Ericsson, Gateway, Fujitsu, IBM, InfoSys (Bangalore), InfoSpace, Intel, Knowledge Universe, Lotus Development Corp (acquired by IBM), Lucent Technologies, MCI, Microsoft, Microland (Bangalore), Motorola, Nokia, Netscape, NEC, Novel, Northern Telecom, Oracle, Pacific Bell (later acquired by SBC Communications), Pacific Century CyberWorks (Hong Kong), RealNetworks, SBC Communications, Siemens, Silicon Graphics, Softbank, Sony, Sprint, Sun Microsystems, Telenor (Norway), Telstra (Australia), United Communications (Thailand), 3Com, Quest, Viacom.

Outside high-tech fields, a few other companies were included. I interviewed only non-IT corporations known to be highly involved in the movement to close the digital divide, particularly financial companies (Goldman Sachs, Citicorp,

Deutsche Bank, and Charles Schwab), and IT-oriented consulting firms (Accenture, McKinsey & Co. and Gartner Group). Interviews were also extended to the philanthropic representatives of Internet titans Bill Gates, Craig McCaw, Jeff Bezos, Rob Glaser, and Paul Allen. Though private foundations' activity was not a central focus of this study, it seemed important to inquire into the non-corporate donations of corporate CEOs to gain a complete view of their philanthropic perspectives.[13]

Parallel to contacting individual companies, the author spoke with leaders of high-tech associations, nonprofit intermediaries, and grantmaking foundations, as well as intergovernmental task forces involved with digital divide issues. In particular, we sought out nonprofit leaders who are considered trusted advisors to their corporate associates.[14]

Three Questions, Three Answers

In order to elucidate why and how the companies were creating **significant** social initiatives, interviews focused on three sets of questions:

- Which major social initiatives have been (or are being) created by these companies?
- Are these projects managed as *philanthropic* enterprises, as expressions of business, or as a combination of both?
- How are high-tech corporate ties to nonprofit organizations *changing* in light of the preeminent role the Internet is playing in corporate strategies?

Regarding the nature of corporate citizenship in the target companies, three conclusions can be briefly stated:

---

[13] For a perspective on the private giving of high-tech moguls, see the writings of Steve Kirsch, founder of the InfoSeek search engine, which he sold to Disney for $200 million, donating a large share of profits to charity. For his insightful essays on digital philanthropy, see www.kirschfoundation.org.

[14] These include Aspen Institute Communications and Society Program, Benton Foundation, Business Software Alliance, Business Council for Sustainable Development, Center for Democracy and Technology, Digital Opportunity Task Force, Information Society (Brazil), Harvard Center for International Development, Internet Policy Institute, W.K. Kellogg Foundation, International Telecommunications Union, Joint Venture: Silicon Valley, Markle Foundation, Media Lab Asia, Morino Institute, MIT Media Lab, Media Lab Asia, New Profit, Inc., Social Venture Partners (Seattle), Technology Alliance (Seattle), World Bank (*info*Dev), UNDP, UNESCO, United Nations ICT Task Force, World Resources Institute (DigitalDividend.org.), World Links for Development.

- **"Signature Initiatives"**[15] **stand out**. Many of the companies have formulated large, high-profile multiyear social initiatives, and most continue despite the downturn in technology markets since mid-2000. Some of these initiatives go beyond the well-established trend of "strategic corporate philanthropy" in which philanthropic initiatives are shaped that add value to business but which are not actually linked to core operations. Some of the new social initiatives can be understood as internal businesses in their own right, which, after an extended period of internal incubation, could conceivably emerge as modest profit centers. By 2002, only one of these projects, a subsidiary of Telenor called Grameen Phone, has achieved profitability.
- **Middle management plays a strategic role**. Although these initiatives stand apart from conventional business practices, they do reflect the changing management innovations practiced by these companies. Indeed, they are an expression of the nonstop reinvention of these companies, driven not from the headquarters level but from their middle ranks.[16] In fact, high-tech companies appear to be expanding their relationships with nonprofit organizations in a way that is distributed through many different business units and functions. The interviews showed that five internal business units generally play a starring role in these alliances, and each provides a separate "lens" through which one can view the increasingly powerful role that nonprofits are playing in corporate strategies now that the Internet is a driver of change. These units are community relations, marketing, human resources, government relations, and research. Understanding why these units are reaching out to nonprofit organizations makes it easier to discern the underlying dynamics that may lead a company to establish signature initiatives. Indeed, it is easy to

---

[15] For a discussion on this term, see p. 15.
[16] See also discussion on p. 23.

imagine why some CEOs may conclude that such projects make sound business sense. Despite NASDAQ's ups and downs, one can imagine that more such efforts will be created.

- **The leadership responds to the digital divide**. Managerial perspectives alone do not explain the scope and scale of the signature initiatives. Leadership is also involved, and CEOs play a subtle but crucial role. The worldwide movement to close the digital divide has presented Internet companies with an opportunity to formulate responses to critics of the role of multinational corporations in society. These days, the most troublesome critics are those in the anti-globalization movement, who point to the unfairness of a world in which a handful of corporations are in the driver's seat of global change. Rather than merely join task forces set up to respond to the digital divide, many high-tech corporations feel pressured to develop their own signature response. During this investigation, many companies involved in this study have flip-flopped from a defensive posture towards digital divide issues to a new stance in which they seek to position themselves as leaders in this global movement. Increasingly, companies see the business advantage in joining forces in cooperative efforts with governments and nonprofit leaders. They hope to reduce the risks entailed in building Internet markets in the developing world and, they hope, to reduce the vehemence of the new anticorporate activists.

CHAPTER TWO

The Rise of "Signature Initiatives"

There is no generally accepted name for the big-ticket corporate social initiatives created in the past few years by high-tech companies. But perhaps "signature initiatives" fits best.[17] Though the initiatives serve multiple purposes that correspond to the distinct motives that propel various internal business units, their larger purpose is to personify the overall corporate brand identity or "signature." Thus, it could be said that the underlying purpose of these initiatives is to help these companies rise above the constant upheavals–implosions, mergers and reinventions–that seem to undermine any semblance of normalcy.[18] "It is a way of healing the company," said one executive at WorldCom, describing the company's long-standing signature initiative called "Marco Polo,"[19] which was originally created by MCI. In fact, all of these initiatives are multiyear ventures, and many of them have impressive staying power.

From AT&T to Cisco: A Proliferation of Initiatives

The granddaddy of all signature initiatives is the AT&T Learning Network, a $150 million[20] internal joint venture designed in 1996 to help America's public schools get connected

---

[17] Of the 60 companies interviewed for this report, approximately half have designated "flag-ship" or "signature" initiatives.

[18] The role of corporate citizenship as an aspect of a company's "brand management" has been a theme at the Conference Board, a membership organization serving senior managers, for at least a decade. Use of high-profile initiatives to define and defend the overall corporate reputation or "brand" is a dominant theme within the Board's Council on Corporate Brands.

[19] Interview with MCI Vice President Diane Strahn 1998. See www.marcopolo.worldcom.com.

[20] The dollar figures indicated here for AT&T and other companies listed in this report were not independently verified. They were conveyed by interviewees or published in promotional literature of the companies.

to the Internet, and then find ways to use the Internet to improve the quality of instruction. It was the first example of a company's marriage between its philanthropic foundation (which contributed $50 million) and its marketing unit, which gave the remaining $100 million. Even after AT&T split itself into separate companies and went through a fundamental overhaul of its management structure, AT&T Learning Network remains a beacon of constancy for the workforce of the venerable, but beleaguered, company.[21]

Signature initiatives like AT&T's emerged in telecommunications beginning in the mid-1990s. Social activists noted alarmingly that the advent of the "new information infrastructure" was disproportionately benefiting the wealthy. Fearing that these concerns would bring onerous new regulations, tele-communications companies, often under the impetus of their Washington, DC, offices, created sizable initiatives that brandished the "digital opportunities" presented by the brave new world of networked communications.[22]

The first such efforts were directed to the field of public education, and they all eventually addressed the challenge of connecting the schools to cable and, eventually, to the Internet. The notion of hooking up the schools as a good way to win favor with regulators was first demonstrated by a remarkable industry effort called "Cable in the Classroom," created in 1989, valued at more than $500 million in mostly in-kind support, and considered one of the largest and most successful corporate-support social collaborations in history.[23]

The list of initiatives included a commitment by Lucent Technologies ($10 million) to promote math and science education to students from low-income backgrounds, and WorldCom embarked on a its long-term Marco Polo project to create Internet curriculum in various subject areas that could be downloaded by any school at no charge. Some companies,

---

[21] See att.com/learningnetwork.
[22] For a lengthier description of the impact of regulatory struggles on the pattern of corporate citizenship in the telecommunications industry, see *Giving by Industry*, edited by Craig Smith, Aspen Publishers, 1999.
[23] For the latest perspectives on Cable in the Classroom (CIC), see www.cicon-line.com.

such as Intel, chose to focus support to education as a philanthropic activity, and Intel eventually devoted as much as $100 million per year in donations for math and science.[24] Verizon brought together all its disparate units in an effort to employ its technology to fight illiteracy. Some companies followed the pattern set earlier by Apple Computer of supporting public schools as a market-development activity. For example, Oracle made no apologies about the marketing agenda behind its $50 million in-kind gift program to put its "networked computers" into "every school in America," which called attention to Oracle's support for networked computers as a digital platform for schools.

In creating their schools initiatives, companies pondered whether to fund their efforts out of their philanthropic budgets or to tap marketing budgets. Most companies, like AT&T, eventually settled on a combined approach in which philanthropic funds and marketing funds would be cojoined. Many combined outright research grants with lavish product donations. They put together internal "market-development" teams that sought tech-based solutions to problems faced by schools. The marriage of marketing and philanthropy proved sufficient to justify major public schools commitments by BellSouth ($100 million) and SBC Communications ($200 million).

IBM added a higher level of sophistication to this formula in its "IBM Reinventing Education" project, created in 1997, which addressed the role of technology in the total reform of entire school districts, each of which received $1 million cash grants. The program, which cost $35 million as of 2000, never reached the enormous scale of those of the telecommunications companies, but it may well have won the company a greater level of prestige in education and government circles. IBM also broke with the pattern of other high-tech companies by linking its initiative to its powerful research units. "We offered schools as a testing ground for our researchers to try out cutting-edge new technology, such as voice recognition software adapted to the voices of children at different age levels," proudly stated Robin Willner, of IBM Community Relations.[25]

---

[24] See www.intel.com/education/programs/html.
[25] Interview at IBM headquarters, 1998.

Eventually, companies branched out beyond the K-12 education field to address other social causes. Typically, dot-coms that focused on niche markets embraced the causes that were closely aligned with those markets; for example, iVillage, the women's portal, chose domestic violence. NetNoir, a portal that gears its content to African-American audiences, chose empowerment of African-Americans; Planet Out, the on-line site for gays, chose AIDS. But for the major Internet portals, the fit between causes and business strategy was less obvious and required careful consideration. eBay, the on-line auctioneer, eventually chose as its target cause senior citizens, an audience segment that was potentially a huge customer base for eBay but which required a focused effort at market development. eBay put together an internal coalition linking the company's marketers, employee volunteers, and its own foundation to encourage the elderly to come on-line. "We want to show how low-income senior citizens can tap eBay's auction site to improve their economic circumstances," said company spokesman Rebecca Guerra.[26]

A number of companies, following a pattern set by MCI's sponsorship of the American Library Association in 1996, embraced libraries as the perfect information-age cause. For example, Microsoft made a mammoth software pledge to public libraries (retail value: $200 million) as part of its Libraries Online! initiative, which has since been transformed into a billion-dollar library and education initiative advanced by the Bill and Melinda Gates Foundation.[27]

Still other signature initiatives are those announced by 3Com, Novel, Oracle, Bertelsmann Foundation, and Microsoft to address the shortage of workers in information technology, which included outreach efforts to the jobless poor in disadvantaged areas.

---

[26] Telephone interview, 2000.

[27] The subject of the Gates Foundation's relationship, or lack of one, to Microsoft, co-founded by Bill Gates, III, is a sensitive one. Gates Foundation spokespersons have been explicit in claiming that the programming of the private foundation, with no formal ties to Microsoft, does not "partner" with the company. The library program was developed by the company and eventually adopted by the foundation. In subsequent programming, the foundation has been vigilant in steering a course that is free of any linkage with the company.

Some dot-coms chose not to support a specific cause but instead supported all nonprofits as a broad category, without discriminating between them. For example, Yahoo! invited nonprofits to come together in a kind of boot camp training called Camp Yahoo! Others went further in taking on the role long associated with nonprofit intermediary organizations by helping their customers connect to their causes. The pioneer in this respect is iVillage.com, which appealed to the values of its on-line women customers by devoting its web site to resources designed to help them find jobs, improve their wellness, fight domestic violence, or overcome the hurdles involved in getting financing for their small businesses. iVillage also pioneered the effort to match volunteers with volunteer opportunities, a theme which was embraced and developed by much more powerful web portals, such as America Online, now AOL Time Warner.

AOL Time Warner remains the most ambitious of the companies seeking to position themselves as brokers between givers and receivers. In its efforts to serve as matchmaker between companies and nonprofits, it offers all nonprofits the opportunity to gain access to any of its millions of members, or even nonmembers who log onto the AOL site. It established a program that claimed to link any of its members to volunteer opportunities in their hometowns. (All that is required is inputting one's ZIP Code, and "voila!"–a list of nonprofit volunteer organizations appears.) The company later extended the method to allow members to use credit cards to make donations to the charities of their choice. Such an approach to matching givers and receivers, challenging the decades-old approach developed by United Way, is clearly emerging as a market opportunity for the companies involved. [28]

---

[28] Believing predictions of a massive and sudden shift towards on-line giving, many investors capitalized a number of companies, hoping to cash in on the phenomenon. Among the "click to donate" sites are GreaterGood.com, which ceased operations in mid-2001amid the crash of dot-coms. Other matchmakers include DonationDepot, DonorNet, and AllCharities. Few individual nonprofits have succeeded in shifting their giving on-line as of 2001. One of the most successful in this effort, the American Red Cross, generated on-line only $2.2 million of the $637 million it raised in 2000, according to the *Chronicle of Philanthropy*. Not a profit-making activity today, the effort to match givers and receivers on-line is potentially a hugely lucrative activity for intermediaries charging small transaction fees.

Another hallmark of signature initiatives is that they often involve a sponsoring company's key business-to-business partners, as well as its nonprofit partners. For example, in its high-profile project to wire schools in the southeastern United States, Bell South collaborated with suppliers, such as Lucent Technologies, whose foundation contributed $3 million to the project. Similarly, Microsoft involved the major laptop manufacturers in "Anytime, Anywhere Learning," an effort to show the educational value of laptop computers for students from disadvantaged backgrounds. At the same time, Microsoft has shown itself willing to reciprocate by joining the signature initiatives of its own corporate partners. Honoring its long-term ties with its "Wintel" partner Intel, it supports the $100 million "Intel Teach to the Future" signature initiative, through which the chip maker intends to train 400,000 classroom teachers in 20 countries worldwide by 2003.

Not all signature initiatives emerge from within companies that end up sponsoring them. Sometimes, nonprofit grantseekers, having studied the business-to-business alliances of a high-tech company, shape social initiatives that help companies establish business-to-business alliances. For example, the American Red Cross induced IBM to sponsor ARC's web site, which generates public response to disasters around the world. At the same time, the Red Cross enlisted for the same project two media companies that were being courted by IBM's marketers: CNN and Gannet's *USA Today*. Both media companies agreed to draw the public's attention to the IBM-sponsored site during times of disaster and, in this way, a corporate coalition was born.

Cisco Systems Points the Way

What the previously mentioned initiatives *don't* show is how such a project can first arise within a high-tech company, gain internal traction, attract external partners, and eventually emerge as a force to be reckoned with both inside the company and in the society at large. A reason is that most of these initiatives, at the time of this writing, are no more than five years old. It may be too soon to gauge their scope and impact. However, if one were to name the single initiative that offers a clue to their potential impact, on the companies that created them and on society, it would be the effort created in 1998 called the Cisco Networking Academies.

The project's origins were both modest and strictly philanthropic. It grew from Cisco's participation that year in "NetDays"[29] in which dozens of high-tech companies wired classrooms to the Internet. As volunteer participants in the effort, Cisco's engineers argued that the core problem wasn't hooking classrooms to the Internet. The real challenge, they said, was to interconnect the classrooms of a school into a coherent and self-sustaining network. Soon, these employee volunteers devised a plan to train high school kids in a comprehensive 280-hour course. Cisco did not have to create the approach from scratch. It was adapted from the company's own certification training programs.

By the end of 2001, the company reported that 100 Cisco employees were employed full-time administering the effort, at a cost of $120 million. At the same time, the national program went global with dizzying speed. In nearly 7,000 locations, the program has enrolled a whopping 150,000 students in all 50 U.S. states and 121 countries.[30] Not yet four years old, the initiative has become the most broadly distributed corporate citizenship initiative in the world.

It is important to note that though Cisco claims to have spent a great deal of money on the program, the company has been able to attract at least that amount in matching funds from various partners, mostly foundations and government agencies, who have been eager to be associated with the prestigious Silicon Valley company. (In fact, Cisco refuses to launch an Academies program without a funding partner to pay for equipment and training.) Insiders in the world of sponsorship will quickly recognize Cisco's strategy as "cross-marketing," in which two partners both gain an advantage from promoting each other's products. George Soros' Open Society Institute, for example, brought the Cisco academies into Eastern

---

[29] See www.netday.org.
[30] See www.cisco.com/warp/public/779/edu/academy.

and Central Europe, and they quickly became a cornerstone of the foundation's effort to build Internet-based "open societies" in that region. The United Nations Development Programme, for its part, pledged to help bring the program into each of the least developed 48 nations. This tie-in promises to give the initiative a global sweep that no other corporate initiative can match.

To justify continuing infusions of cash from within the company while at the same time arguing for matching funds from philanthropic organizations, the company has had to carefully delineate its "business case" from its "philanthropic case"–stressing one point of view internally and another in discussions to the outside world. Its nonprofit partners seem to understand that Cisco has to walk a fine line in its justification of the program. "From a philanthropic perspective, the initiative serves dual purposes. First, it boosts the careers of student trainees, many from disadvantaged backgrounds, who become quickly employable right after high school. Second, it fills a gaping hole in the technology-in-schools programs, which typically lack technicians able to develop and update school networks," said James Lanier, the former director of Los Angeles Country's Technology-in-Schools program, in which Cisco Network Academies is deeply involved.[31]

At the same time, Mr. Lanier suspects Cisco's investment is clearly justifiable to the company as a business expense. "It's a way they can leverage the certification programs they have already developed. It helps them with marketing to educational institutions. It gives them a way that their employees can be involved in a morale-boosting project. And it is undoubtedly impressive to regulators."

A common perception about the Networking Academies is that graduates go on to become employees of Cisco. But company spokeswoman Christine Hemrick claims that is not true. She argues that the program boosts the human resources of Cisco's business *clients*–not the human resources of Cisco itself. "Very few Cisco employees are graduates of the program,"

---

[31] Interview in Los Angeles, 1998.

she said. "Cisco's growth depends on the steady supply of trained Internet technicians who know how to build networks."[32]

And the final sign of success is that there is now so much momentum behind the Cisco Networking Academy Program that it has taken on an economic life of its own. When interviewed in 2001, Ms. Hemrick was mulling options for spinning off the Academy program as an independent freestanding company, which could be adapted to the needs of all sorts of institutions and government agencies.

CEOs in the Back Seat

One factor that sets apart Cisco's Academy from corporate leadership projects of the past is that CEO John Chambers, one of the highest profile executives in business history, is barely involved. In fact, today's corporate chiefs as a whole play a minor role in the development and implementation of these efforts. Among companies that are market leaders today, few CEOs are social activists of the sort who were legendary in past decades. One does not find a counterpart to, for example, Robert O. Andersen, the Atlantic Richfield CEO who led the rebuilding of Los Angeles after the ethnic unrest of the 1970s. The dot-com world never generated activist CEOs like William Norris, the founder of Control Data Corp., whose impassioned plea for "turning America's most pressing unmet needs into business opportunities" caused a stir in corporate America in the 1980s. (Though Mr. Norris founded Control Data, he was eventually replaced by his own disgruntled board members, who complained of his "social adventurism.")

Certainly, there was a high level of philanthropic involvement in the 1980s and early 1990s among the CEOs of the "Seven Sister" mainframe computer makers. IBM CEO John Akers spent nearly a quarter of his time in some years tending to his memberships on nonprofit boards of directors.[33] But by

---

[32] Conversation at Cisco headquarters, 2001.
[33] At the time of his retirement from IBM in 1993, Akers had chaired or assumed leadership roles in most of the blue chip nonprofit causes that had been embraced by corporate America, including United Way of America, the National Urban League, National Action Program for Minorities in Engineering, and Council for Aid to Education.

the late 1990s, such CEOs had been replaced by business leaders who were more narrowly focused on their core businesses. According to Becky Morgan, President of Joint Venture: Silicon Valley, "The generation of 'ambassadorial CEOs' is being replaced by younger chief executives who are often so constrained by the competitive pressures that surround them that they are forced to spend less time than their predecessors addressing social concerns."[34]

Certainly, there are exceptions to that Silicon Valley pattern, labeled "cyberselfish" by Paulina Boorsook in her book damning the self-involvement of the *digerati*.[35] Notably, the CEO of San Jose's Applied Materials, James Morgan, has been the leader behind many of Silicon Valley's efforts to resolve social problems that resulted from the region's nonstop growth.[36] In 1996, John Akers' successor at IBM, Lou Gerstner, distinguished himself by convening a major IBM summit on education reform, attracting the President of the United States, 41 governors, and a host of CEOs, including IBM's direct competitors.[37] Two years later, America Online's Steve Case did the same sort of thing– He presided over a "Children's Summit" in Washington, DC, to generate public/private cooperation on Internet issues that affect children. But, following the pattern of diminished executive involvement on social issues, neither CEO has been as visible on social issues in the years since.

Though corporate insiders regret the lack of CEO involvement, others applaud that fact and explain that only when top executives get out of the way are they able to create initiatives that can make a difference and be sustained over the long haul. "It's the CEO's job to create the environment that makes these initiatives happen," says Diane Strahn, who formerly headed WorldCom's foundation. "But it is increasingly

---

[34] Interview in San Francisco, 1998.

[35] See www.cyberselfish.com.

[36] Morgan was a founder of Charitech, a visionary Silicon Valley initiative to introduce high-tech companies to nonprofits needing corporate supporters in Silicon Valley. He also was a creator of Joint Venture: Silicon Valley, which went far beyond a typical chamber of commerce in serving as a source for public/private partnership in addressing the economic and social needs of the Valley.

[37] The education summit later became a semiannual event, in its forth year by 2001, and Mr. Gerstner still figures prominently in its agenda. See www.ibm.com/lvg/1009.phtml.

the job of middle and senior managers to come up with the ideas for programs and carry them out. They are the ones who are in a position to carefully design a social initiative so that it is consistent with our business objectives. It creates the possibility that philanthropic considerations can be integrated directly into the operations of the company. CEOs are operating at a level where they are unable to play that role."[38]

Management

Signature initiatives typically represent an internal alliance of managers from different departments, most commonly:
- community relations
- marketing
- human resources management
- government relations
- research

By examining recent trends in each of these five functions, it becomes possible to understand how public-interest considerations are surfacing within the business strategies of high-tech companies, creating conditions for signature initiatives. Out of these internal collaborations, companies gain the wherewithal to serve short-term goals, even while they formulate visionary leadership efforts on a broad issue, such as the digital divide. This analysis suggests that, for different reasons, each of these five functions is moving towards ever-deepening involvement with nonprofit organizations, even during times of economic downturn. Signature initiatives emerge when managers in one or more of these functions come together and find ways to meet multiple objectives at the same time.

[38] Conversation at MCI headquarters, 1998.

How traditional corporate philanthropy in high-tech companies is being reinvented

➤ Corporate contributions managers have restructured their philanthropy programs so that they focus their time and money increasingly on those nonprofits able to make the most innovative use of their companies' technology for social purposes.

➤ Though education is the major focus of high-tech corporate giving, the theme of education is not confined to K-12 education; it extends to integrating educational dimensions into many other nonprofit fields, for example health education, environmental education, job training, and so on.

➤ Technology has become a "linchpin" theme linking giving programs to business units, and companies often use nonprofits to identify the most visionary applications of a company's cutting-edge technologies.

➤ Contributions managers often see themselves as matchmakers between nonprofit leaders and internal managers who are able to provide more substantial funding. In fact, the contributions managers now spend a third of their time responding to managers in other departments who want to form their own ties with nonprofit organizations.

➤ As high-tech corporate donors became more strategic in their giving, the budget levels of their philanthropy programs rose. Furthermore, the extent of their companies' overall ties with nonprofit organizations also increased.

Corporate Community Relations in Digital Companies

The Philanthropic Dimension

Though high-tech corporations no longer view corporate philanthropy as the only expression of their support of social causes, it is nonetheless true that in-house professionals who oversee the companies' charitable donations have played a crucial role in the formulation of their companies' signature initiatives. As in the case of the Cisco Networking Academy Program, initiatives that began as voluntary or philanthropic efforts were later "picked up" by a marketing unit or an executive office, which scaled it up and broadened its scope. In other cases, the contributions officers served as mere matchmakers and advisors, helping the business units establish their own relationships with nonprofit organizations.

That corporate contributions managers now see their role as catalysts for integrating social issues into overall corporate management is at the heart of "strategic corporate philanthropy," which in the past 15 years has remained the dominant trend[39] in the field of corporate philanthropy.[40] The new approach represented a sea-change in thinking. Up until the 1980s, corporate giving was only considered a legitimate activity if it were on behalf of causes unrelated to the donor company's

---

[39] The first analysis of the paradigm of strategic corporate philanthropy was in *Harvard Business Review*, "The New Corporate Philanthropy," by Craig Smith, *HBR*, May/June, 1994. See also a Conference Board report, "Doing Good by Doing Well, Making the Business Case for Corporate Citizenship," November, 2000. Report #R-1282-00-RR. Order through www.conferenceboard.org.

[40] In-house philanthropic professionals have various corporate titles and work through several different philanthropic structures, for example "corporate community affairs" departments and "corporate foundations."

business interests and conducted at arm's length.[41] But that has changed. "Our goal is to help internal business units make their own ties with nonprofit organizations so that, over time, we would achieve synergy between what we are doing through our foundation and our core business strategies," said Diane Strahn, former executive director of the MCI Foundation.[42]

In most companies, the shift towards a more strategic approach to giving has occurred slowly over a number of years. One way to view the impact of the Internet on this field is that it has accelerated the process by which corporate giving officers achieve synergy between their companies' business strategy and their philanthropy. To understand why a company's giving professionals may want to tear down the walls that remain between philanthropy and business, it is worthwhile to review the evolution of corporate giving since the mid-1980s. During this period, corporate philanthropy shifted from being an ad hoc function performed out of the CEO's office to being a professionally managed activity, just like any other function of business. If there was a historic moment that defined the new approach to corporate giving, it had to be the AT&T divestiture in 1982, after which a new AT&T Foundation broke with tradition by declaring that it would no longer serve as the company's ambassador to "the community." Instead of simply representing the company to nonprofit organizations, the foundation said that it would serve the company as well by being as its "eyes and ears" in the nonprofit sector. "We felt we could serve the company by helping it adjust its marketing and human resources policies in light of the ideas surfacing within the nonprofit sector," said Reynold Levy, who was the new foundation's first president.[43] Soon, Bell Atlantic, US West, Bell South and other regional Bell operating companies fell in line by concentrating

---

[41] In the 1950s and 1960s, regulations at the state and federal levels in the U.S. were gradually relaxed and incentives were created that allow businesses to make tax-deductible gifts even though these were not related to their business purpose. Outside the United States, many nations continue to discourage corporate philanthropy through their regulatory frameworks.
[42] Interview in Washington, DC, 1998.
[43] Interview with Levy in *Corporate Philanthropy Report*, 1988. See also Levy's reflection on his experience with the AT&T Foundation and his perspective on strategic corporate philanthropy in *Give and Take: A Candid Account of Corporate Philanthropy*, Harvard Business School Press, 1999.

their donations on themes that were closely aligned with their business interests, as did a non-Bell competitor, GTE. In 1995, when MCI (now WorldCom) emerged with a significant share of the long distance telephone market, it revamped its giving to focus totally on Internet projects.

In the computer industry, IBM played a trend-setting role analogous to that of AT&T in telecommunications. A difference is that in 1980s, Big Blue (IBM) chose not to create a separate corporate foundation. "It would have forced the company to conduct its giving at arm's length from its core businesses," said Jack Sabatar, formerly IBM community relations director.[44] Instead of erecting a Chinese wall between philanthropy and business, IBM became the first major high-tech company to make its own technology the dominant theme of its business interests. Furthermore, the community relations department conducted research that determined that employee volunteerism was an important tool for building morale and teamwork among its employees. This research led to a broad alignment between the company's human resources (HR) department and its community relations department, setting in motion a close linkage between corporate philanthropy and corporate volunteerism.[45] For example, the HR department added specific questions to the annual employee survey about employees' interests in various causes. The community relations department used the information to diligently tailor its giving programs to employee interests, even to the point of targeting IBM's educational support to the grade levels (middle schools) that were identified by employees as most needing help. Eventually, the IBM community relations department became the first of its kind to attempt to quantify the contribution that it was making to the company by supporting policies for morale-building and retention of the company's workforce.

IBM's was also the first major corporate giving program to emphasize the role of its technology as a way of improving the

---

[44] Interview with Sabatar in *Corporate Philanthropy Report*, 1991.
[45] "Desperately Seeking Data: Why Research Is Crucial to the New Corporate Philanthropy" in *Corporate Philanthropy at the Crossroads*, edited by Dwight F. Burlingame and Dennis R. Young, Indiana University Press, 1996, pp. 1-6.

management efficiency of nonprofit organizations. Initially, this theme was applied to universities, which typically received the bulk of IBM's support, and IBM sponsored many projects that encouraged innovative approaches to automating the administrative functions of higher education institutions. The technology theme was soon replicated in the giving programs of IBM's competitors–especially Digital Equipment Corporation, Hewlett-Packard, Control Data, and others–who also derived the bulk of profits from sales of mainframe or minicomputers.

It was not until the brash arrival of Apple Computer, however, that it became clear that technology could be a tool for transforming the social change strategies employed by all kinds of nonprofit organizations. Playing David to IBM's Goliath, Apple called attention to ways that the personal computer could empower the thousands of grassroots and activist groups that had proliferated wildly since the 1970s. By the mid-1980s, Apple brought activists to its Cupertino headquarters, gave them modems and software, and taught them to collaborate through the creation of computer networks. "In these sessions, the idea was born that technology wouldn't just help nonprofits become as efficient as for-profit organizations, but that there were visionary new uses of technology that nonprofits were in the best position to implement," said Fred Silverman, Apple's community relations manager.[46]

Another way that Apple Computer brought innovation into the corporate citizenship practices of computer companies was through its lavish program of computer donations to public schools. However, when Apple's fortunes sagged in the early 1990s, its community relations program of support to nonprofits was drastically curtailed. Since then, it has not announced a signature initiative that drew upon all parts of the company, and it largely ceased to introduce management innovations into its corporate citizenship practices.

---

[46] Interview in *Corporate Philanthropy Report*, 1993.

Microsoft Weighs In

In 1996 Microsoft's community affairs department launched the most extensive strategic planning process ever attempted by a community relations department of a Fortune 500 company. It was a time when Microsoft's management structure was closely studied and imitated among new and old companies of the Fortune 500. Up through the mid-1990s, it was by no means clear that Bill Gates was going to follow the corporate philanthropy pattern of his father, who had been a pace-setter in Seattle's corporate philanthropy networks.[47] (In his role as a prominent lawyer and volunteer with the Greater Seattle Chamber of Commerce, Bill Gates the elder had advocated that big companies such as Boeing and Safeco give two percent of their pretax profits in hard funds to charity–a level of cash giving that Microsoft has not come close to attaining.) Bill Gates, the young CEO, had clearly rejected the pattern of corporate-philanthropy boosterism encouraged by Boeing, Wayerhaeuser, and other Seattle companies. "He was known to rudely rebuff calls by CEOs who, in effect, said "I'll fund your cause if you'll fund mine," said one manager, on condition of anonymity. As late as 1996, Bill Gates was not prominently involved in any of the established corporate causes. (United Way was the single exception. Bill Gates' mother, Mary Gates, has been a dedicated volunteer for United Way for decades. She easily won the endorsement of her son to her favorite cause.)

Until 1996, the most distinguishing feature of Microsoft's philanthropy was that it put the company's employees in the driver's seat. Gates' policy was to provide a one-to-one match of the giving of any employee–not just managers and executives as was common in most companies with matching gifts policies. The policy was considered highly progressive and generous as an employee-relations gesture,[48] but it had the unintended effect of robbing Microsoft of any overarching policy direction

---

[47] Interview with Bill Gates, Sr., Seattle, 2001.
[48] Of companies that provide a one-to-one match for employees, a typical ceiling for matching gifts is usually in the range of $3000. For details on matching gifts, see the Council for Aid to Education (www.case.org/matchinggifts).

for its support of causes. By the mid-1990s, the company had only a very few strategically important relationships with nonprofits, conducted out of various departments–for example, the company's research department supported the digitalization of the library at Carnegie Mellon University; government affairs supported Washington think tanks, such as the Center for Technology and Society. But the company had no central repository of information and expertise on the nonprofit sector and no sense of how nonprofits might fit into Microsoft's overall strategic business agenda, even though Microsoft as a whole was already considered a major driver of change in society as a whole.[49]

Recognizing that it was time to find a strategic alignment between Microsoft's business interests and its support of nonprofit organizations, Gates decided in 1996 to hire Barbara Dingfield, a Seattle housing executive who had recently led a radical management restructuring of the local United Way. She became the company's first contributions professional. Ms. Dingfield focused on discerning the strategic challenges facing managers in each of these units–Microsoft Network, the desktop software division, including its Microsoft Office suite of software, the operating systems division, its multimedia products, and so on–and then investigating whether nonprofit organizations could be useful to these divisions. The assessment yielded the surprising conclusion that dozens of relationships had spontaneously emerged within the company, without the guiding hand of any policy directive from headquarters. Some inside the company called these nonprofit projects "random acts of kindness."

All this research led the company to eventually create a policy framework that called for a two-tiered structure, similar to that of other companies: The company would continue to support a wide variety of nonprofit organization in response to requests from employees, customers and civic leaders. At the same time, it would establish a more proactive and more centrally managed approach on behalf of "flagship" social

---

[49] See *The Making of Microsoft*, Daniel Ichbiah and Susan Knepper, *PRIMA*, 1991, pp. 222-226.

initiatives built around each of three themes: entrepreneurship, learning, and creativity. The idea was to develop large multiyear programs to advance each of these three causes and to do so in a way that would offer Microsoft's technology, its cash donations, and its expertise. Rather than conduct these programs out of Microsoft's own headquarters, the company outsourced much of the work to big nonprofits, such as the American Library Association, which served not only as a buffer against fears of Microsoft's commercial agenda but also as a distribution channel that could eventually be used to reach local affiliates in thousands of cities and towns.

For example, in support of its focus on "entrepreneurship," the company found a willing partner in the American Association of Community Colleges. The initiative was a $30 million five-year program called "Working Connections," which boosted the technological capacities and curricula in community colleagues, targeting some of the country's most impoverished community colleges.

Such flagship programs not only made sense in philanthropic terms–they clearly concentrated on a few causes where Microsoft was able to add value–but they also had the important effect inside Microsoft of establishing an unusual level of prominence for Ms. Dingfield and her small professional staff. Rarely are in-house philanthropists given a seat at the table in policy discussions. But at Microsoft the community relations department was known as a "knowledge unit," capable of offering insider advice to other departments wanting to have ties to nonprofit organizations. For example, the department's managers were eventually able to serve as a congealing point for various business units involved in the company's support of universities–recruiters, researchers, educational sales units–even though these other internal divisions had budgets many time the size of that for Microsoft's community relations.

As the community relations department grew in status, its budget expanded proportionally to $231 million by 2000, making it the number two corporate donor in the United States (after Coca-Cola), with approximately 80 percent of this amount counted as the retail value of donated software.

Even at its substantial scale, the company's giving became dwarfed by the much larger philanthropy of the Bill & Melinda Gates Foundation, whose endowment jumped to $23 billion by the year 2000. A big subject of speculation in Seattle's nonprofit circles is whether some form of coordination exists between the huge private foundation and the strategic giving program of Microsoft. According to the foundation's president, Patty Stonesifer, there is no such linkage. Nonetheless, it is possible that the strategic framework introduced by the company's community relations department may well have influenced the nature of Bill Gates' private philanthropy.

How Corporate Philanthropists Leverage the Internet

Perhaps because Microsoft's embrace of strategic corporate giving was so dramatic, the trend quickly became established among other software companies that became prominent in the late 1990s boom years when dot-coms captured the imagination. A study conducted by the Community Foundation Silicon Valley in 1994 and again in 1997 confirmed that, in the second time period, the giving programs of the top software companies in the Valley had also established formal management plans and policies for their philanthropic activity. [50] By the late 1990s, most major Internet leaders in the Valley– Cisco, Sun Microsystems, H-P, Silicon Graphics, Advanced MicroDevices, eBay, and Yahoo–had embarked on a strategic planning process similar to the one that Microsoft had conducted. eBay, for example, had established a program that explores how nonprofit organizations and disadvantaged groups could tap the auction site to generate charitable income or reduce social problems. ("In looking ahead to the spread of eBay to the developing world, we want to look ahead to how traditional systems of barter could be strengthened, leading to job growth and cultural preservation," said eBay co-founder Jeff Skoll.[51]) Compaq, Dell and Gateway, though slower to embrace the trend,

---

[50] See "Corporate Community Involvement in Silicon Valley," November 1995 and "Giving Back, The Silicon Valley Way," November 1998, available through the Silicon Valley Community Foundation web site, www.cfsv.org.
[51] Interview in Santa Clara, CA, 2001.

had also taken modest steps towards strategic philanthropy by the late 1990s.

Though companies were eager to tout their initiatives, they also admitted that their efforts were a work in progress, and they admitted that powerful forces inside their companies held back their ability to integrate philanthropy with business. Nonetheless they all conveyed the assurance that this integration would be achieved over time. "We're right at the verge of a seamless integration between our business practices and our philanthropy," said Motorola Senior Vice President Samme Thompson.[52]

It is impossible to gauge the impact of strategic corporate philanthropy on a company's giving levels. But it should be noted that, during the late 1990s, when high-tech companies embraced the strategic approach to giving, corporate philanthropy rose in double digits, achieving an 18 percent increase in 1999, according to *Giving USA*, which indicated a total level of corporate giving at $11 billion in that year.[53] Even more important, corporate giving levels as a percentage of pretax income also increased during this period, to 1.1 percent of earnings, reversing a long-term decline established in the mid-1980s.

According to a report from the Center for Corporate Citizenship at Boston College, contributions managers themselves claim that their "internal consulting" in their companies is a factor that explains recent budget increases. According to the study of more than 150 contributions managers, these professionals now spend about one-third of their time responding to requests for assistance from other managers inside their companies.[54]

But the more important impact of strategic corporate giving may not be on the philanthropic budgets at all, but on the budgets of other internal departments. Thanks, in part, to the quiet advocacy of strategic giving departments, a wider and wider range of internal business units developed their own ties with nonprofit organizations.

---

[52] Interview at Schaumburg, IL headquarters of Motorola, 2001.

[53] *Giving USA 2000, The Annual Report on Philanthropy,* published by the AAFRC Trust for Philanthropy, 2000. See http://www.aafrc.org.

[54] See Center for Corporate Citizenship at Boston College web site, http://www.bc.edu/bc_org/avp/csom/ccc/index.html.

Why Internet marketers turn to nonprofits

➤ The downturn in technology capital markets of 2000 through 2002 has intensified the search for innovative and interactive approaches to on-line advertising. These new approaches often involve collaborations with nonprofits. Non-advertising forms of marketing (in which nonprofits play a role) are increasing – for example affinity marketing, sponsorships, and cause-related marketing.

➤ Nonprofit tie-ins to these new non-advertising approaches are being formed on behalf of the economically disadvantaged.

➤ Product giveaways are an increasingly important strategy of software and Internet companies, a trend that has great implications for nonprofit organizations serving low-income persons who cannot afford technology.

➤ Market development units are being created to serve as catalysts for new education markets, government markets, developing-country markets and special constituencies' markets (for example ethnic minorities and women).

➤ These units rely heavily on implied endorsements (or quasi-endorsements) from third-party organizations, including governmental and nonprofit organizations.

➤ Efforts to build markets in developing countries involve technology transfer and "intellectual transfer" to help governments achieve reforms in education, economic development, and social services.

➤ A network of digital divide umbrella organizations is emerging to help forge partnerships between international NGOs and corporations in the developing world.

Corporate Marketing by Digital Companies

The Transformation of High-Tech Marketing

To understand how nonprofit organizations are gaining a foothold in high-tech corporate marketing departments, it is important to understand two overarching trends in Internet marketing practices frequently mentioned by commentators.

One trend is the transformation of these corporations from "engineering corporations" (that happen to do marketing) to "marketing corporations" (that happen to have engineers on the payroll). Increasingly, the expertise of the high-tech workforce lies not in the production of merchandise but in less tangible activities–like creating markets where there were none before and coaxing consumers to buy products they didn't know they needed. Mega-campaigns, like Microsoft's selling of Windows 95, reached out simultaneously to the media, retailers, customers, software developers, and their own employees until this product launch became a cover story in *Time* magazine. Nokia cut Motorola's wireless market share in half in 1999 and 2000 because Nokia marketers had borrowed techniques used successfully by Nike, Sony, and others to create a buzz among teenage consumers. "We once thought we were makers of *things*," says Deborah Dunn, Senior Vice President for Strategy at Hewlett-Packard. "But now we are makers of ideas that empower people. It's a fundamental cultural shift."[55]

A second dimension is that marketing itself is changing in keeping with the enormous influence of the Internet. Marketing is no longer just about advertising and mass media. Instead of

---

[55] Interview at Palo Alto H-P headquarters, 2001.

relying on ad agencies and broadcasters, the digital corporations are becoming media powerhouses in their own right. Their challenge lies close to home–to tap their own technology (which they control) in combination with the Internet (which they don't) in order to instantly appear compelling, hip, and of the moment. Relying on the Internet as a marketing tool has corresponded to bottom-up approaches to building momentum for causes, resulting in an outpouring of books on buzz-marketing and other techniques that convey ways of creating a word-of-mouth effect.[56]

In response to this shift, high-tech firms have gone outside the engineering field to find leaders who understand how to integrate marketing principles into every aspect of the business. This trend is already a decade in the making. A watershed event occurred in 1993 when Lou Gerstner, a marketer from RJR Nabisco, took over the helm of IBM, replacing John Akers, who embodied the engineering ethic at Big Blue. Since then, similar shifts have occurred at dozens of other major high-tech companies, culminating in the most audacious move of all, the arrival at the helm of Yahoo! of a Hollywood studio head, Terry Semel, the long-time Warner Brothers mogul.

These two trends have led to a period of extraordinary experimentation in marketing practices in which nonprofits are frequently involved. All this is happening in an atmosphere of extreme uncertainty. No one is sure which business model for making money via the Internet will eventually surpass the others. Will it be retail sales from products shipped to consumers–or from services delivered on a subscription basis through wireless networks? Maybe it will be from Internet tie-ins to old-economy retailers who continue to operate in much the same way? Or will it be a combination of the above?[57]

---

[56] *The Anatomy of Buzz: How To Create Word of Mouth*, by Emanuel Rosen, Doubleday, 2000.
[57] According to one study, there are two dominant forms of web-based advertising: sponsored content sites, such as CNN and Salon, and entry portal sites, such as Yahoo, that function as gateways to the web and provide search and directory features for Web browsers. Since 2000, with the downturn in NASDAQ, both of these approaches have failed to produce anticipated results, and alternative approaches are being sought with greater vigor. See "E-Loyalty: Your Secret Weapon on the Web," by Frederick Reicheld and Philip Scheter, *Harvard Business Review*, July-August, 2000, pp. 105-113.

An academic duo has given this matter much thought. Donna Hoffman and Thomas Novak run an "e-Lab" from the business school at Vanderbilt University. They have been tracking the evolution of marketing practices since 1996. They note a shift away from passive forms of advertising derived from the old economy, such as "banner ads" on web sites, to more experimental and interactive forms, which may involve partnerships with nonprofit organizations.[58]

Whichever way it will be, the stakes are high. Forrester Research, the company that tracks market trends and technology change, predicts that by 2004, as much as 8 percent of the world's total gross sales will occur on-line, hitting $6.8 trillion in that year, up from about $1 trillion in 2001.[59] Despite such numbers, there are still very few companies making a profit through their on-line commerce, and, given the winner-take-all mentality that dominates the Internet, few companies may be able to profit in the future.[60] With those stakes, the leading on-line competitors can easily afford to involve nonprofits in experimentations that may or may not lead to new approaches to sales.

The key to understanding the role of nonprofits in high-tech marketing practices is to understand that "market development" refers not to sales campaigns but to the relationship-building activity that precedes them. While sales campaigns may have only a few months to show returns on investments, market-development units often have as many as three years for payoff.[61] Even while companies rely on traditional marketing practices for the high-end business-to-business customers, they are hoping innovations in marketing practices will emerge from their market-development units. These units target consumers, such as ethnic minorities, women, seniors, and the handicapped, as

---

[58] "Advertising Pricing Models for the World Wide Web," by Donna Hoffman and Thomas Novak, in *Internet Publishing and Beyond: The Economics of Digital Information and Intellectual Property*, MIT Press, 2000.

[59] See www.forrester.com.

[60] *The Global Advance of Electronic Commerce, Reinventing Markets, Management and National Sovereignty*, by David Bollier, Communications and Society Program, Aspen Institute, 1998.

[61] This is merely a rule of thumb. A market-development process could be as short as 18 months in an example of introducing an item for the advanced market, such as a line of computerized toys. But developing a market for, say, China, may take as long as five years before the effort is expected to show a return.

well as government markets, along with consumers in developing countries–all market segments in which nonprofit tie-ins may be key to customer loyalty.

Companies are willing to spend a great deal to develop relationships that will inspire loyalty among new groups of customers. Another Forrester Research report notes a shakeout in on-line marketing. It claims that as few as 200 companies will ultimately be anointed as premier global on-ramps to the Internet (though thousands or even millions of other companies will be able to service specialized on-line constituencies).[62] These top portals may well become the preferred venues for much of on-line commerce since they will be in a position to aggregate demand across millions, even billions, of consumers. Thus, analysts argue, it is more important for companies to build consumer loyalty now, before the true take-off of on-line commerce, than it is to show a high level of profits–though profits of some kind are indeed *de rigueur* in today's markets. An often expressed goal of on-line marketers is to "build community," a phrase borrowed from civic activists. Jeff Bezos, CEO of Amazon.com, perhaps the most successful practitioner of on-line commerce, has declared that he owes the success of his company to a strategy of community building called "affinity marketing."

A Surge in Affinity Marketing

"Affinity marketing," as a term, was first used in the mid-1980s to describe the cross-marketing relationships formed between credit card companies and nonprofit organizations. For example, VISA and the Audubon Society formed relationships in which they each displayed the other's logo: VISA marketed Audubon's memberships in its advertising to the public, while Audubon marketed VISA to its members. In such cases, the corporate partner was interested not merely in access to the consumers associated with the nonprofit, but also in tapping into the loyalty between the nonprofit and its members.

---

[62] *The eMarketPlace Shakeout*, August 2000, by Steve Kafka, et al., on sale for $595 and downloadable from www.forrester.com.

How affinity marketing fits into digital marketing was first addressed in *Net Gain: Expanding Markets Through Virtual Communities*, by John Hegel, III, and Arthur G. Armstrong.[63] The authors argue that the successful brand builders in the next phase of the digital revolution will be those who build a community experience, a kind of safe shelter from the chaos of the Internet. Loyalty is perhaps the most compelling reason why many companies, engaged in a life-and-death struggle to be the preeminent "portals" to the Internet, are struggling to "build community" on the Net. In this way, they develop a customer base who now may be more comfortable with a switch to on-line purchasing.

One academic study of "e-loyalty" compared old-economy businesses, such as brick and mortar grocery and other retail stores, to such new-economy businesses as consumer electronics that are sold over the Web. The conclusion: "Lack of customer loyalty was a much bigger factor in explaining the failure of Web-based businesses than it was in conventional retail or apparel, which are more price sensitive," said researchers Frederick Reicheld and Philip Sheter.[64]

According to Vanderbilt's Hoffman and Novak, some web advertisers have adopted a variation on the affinity marketing approach called "per inquiry advertisements" in which advertisers pay direct commissions.[65] If a visitor accesses the advertiser through the affiliate's web site and purchases the product advertised on the affiliate's site, the affiliate receives a referral fee or commission. Referrals typically range from $.50 to $5 or more per lead, while commissions range from 10 to 25 percent of the purchase price of the product.

Amazon.com offers an example of a company which established a version of this approach and, in so doing, many have helped to transform the marketing profession itself. As it turns out, nonprofits figure prominently in the approach. In a

---

[63] Harvard Business School Press, 1997.
[64] "E-Loyalty: Your Secret Weapon on the Web," by Frederick Reicheld and Philip Scheter, *Harvard Business Review*, July-August, 2000, pp. 105-113.
[65] "Advertising Pricing Models for the World Wide Web," by Donna Hoffman and Thomas Novak, in *Internet Publishing and Beyond: The Economics of Digital Information and Intellectual Property*, MIT Press, 2000, p.13.

strategy to make Amazon ubiquitous on the Internet, the company created an Associates Program in which Amazon arranged links to other web sites owned by businesses, government agencies, or nonprofit organizations. In this arrangement, an organization such as the National Peace Corps Association, is able to offer books about international issues to Peace Corps alumni. Purchases made via Amazon generate a 15 percent commission for the association.

Public schools represent a particularly important object of Amazon.com's attention. The basic arrangement is similar to the company's arrangement with other businesses: parents and students log onto a school's web site and purchase books (from Amazon), for which the school receives a commission. To encourage more such cross-marketing among schools that lack web sites, Amazon staffers actually create the sites for them. Furthermore, in an effort to build this school-based market, Amazon has created an adjunct marketing program designed to promote literacy for disadvantaged children, called "Books for Kids." "Basically, we help schools build sites that allow the public to donate books on behalf of children from low-income backgrounds whose parents could not afford to buy them. It's a way of updating the traditional notion of a 'book drive,' says Shawn Hayes, who manages "Books for Kids" for Amazon.

Mr. Hayes sees such marketing initiatives as "Books for Kids" as precursors of a possible embrace by Amazon.com of literacy—a cause in which bookstores and publishers have often taken a leadership role. "Though our company has a high stock price, it hasn't yet made a profit, so we are not in a position to donate a share of profits to charity. This is a way that we can make our first steps toward seeing nonprofits as strategic partners," Hayes said.[66]

The Nonprofit Role in Product Giveaways

Giving away freebies or slashing prices to benefit nonprofit organizations is another way that marketing departments employ affinity marketing. Of course, such activity has always been a part of promotion in business. But giveaways are especially prevalent in Internet-based companies, which are

---

[66] Interview in Seattle, 1999.

willing to slash margins or eliminate them altogether in order to win the loyalty of their customers. Furthermore, as technological advances lead to cheaper and more ubiquitous products, and as advertisers become more attracted to the Internet, it becomes possible for digital companies to reconstruct their business models to offer for free, or at far lower cost, the same services or products that they had offered at a substantial fee in the previous year. For example, in 1999, America Online and other on-line service providers experimented with campaigns to offer free personal computers to consumers who were willing to sign long-term contracts for use of their services.

The dramatic nature of the industry's free offerings sometimes catches the world of philanthropy off guard. For example, the notion of free e-mail or "E-Mail for All" was a concept developed by the Markle Foundation and the nonprofit Rand Corporation in 1995. Its proponents, anticipating that ubiquitous e-mail would contribute to federal equity goals, argued that $1 billion per year should be set aside in the United States budget for that purpose. But in the same year, an upstart e-mail company called Juno began to offer free e-mail by transferring costs to advertisers. This practice was later adopted by Yahoo, Hotmail, and other on-line providers.

As companies develop new product lines, they often donate to nonprofits as a way of generating favorable publicity about the benefits of their products. In 1998, AT&T developed a new service called AT&T Language Line, which offered instant language translation services in dozens of languages. When callers dialed in to the service, they were connected to multilingual operators (based in remote locations) who acted as intermediaries, helping the callers communicate over the phone. Recognizing the public-interest value of the service, AT&T quickly offered it at no charge to hospitals, which use it to help healthcare professionals communicate with patients. The in-kind donation could have been justified as a philanthropic contribution by the company, but they preferred to consider it a marketing expense because of the resulting relationships in the healthcare industry. These relationships allowed AT&T to succeed in its marketing to health care professionals.

All Marketers Converge in Public Schools

Schools have been a major focus of the attention of cost-cutting marketers. After Apple Computer won market share in the education market in the early 1980s by offering deep discounts to schools, most other hardware and software vendors followed suit. Microsoft, for example, began its program of "School Technology Nights" that offers its technology at 80 percent of the usual cost to parents and teachers who attend a workshop to learn how the technology can enhance parent-student-teacher relationships.

In the early 1990s, cable companies offered widespread free hook-ups for schools in their operating areas, and they sometimes offered curriculum guides along with free cable use for a specific period of time. The cable industry claims that nearly $500 million worth of services have been provided to schools involved in the industry's "Cable in the Classroom" initiative alone.

Over time, as the education market has continued to expand, most major high-tech companies have established independent divisions addressing education consumers. According to the *Wall Street Journal*, Internet access in public schools continues to rise, up 77 percent in 2000, compared to 64 percent in 1999.[67] As educational marketing becomes more important, companies such as Knowledge Universe, Inc. are preparing to compete in educational service delivery at the K-12 level and have enlisted nonprofits to support their competitive strategies. In order to legitimize his challenge of conventional educational practices, chairman (of Knowledge Universe) Michael Milken has enlisted William Bennet, former Secretary of the Department of Education, to develop a complete on-line K-12 school, to demonstrate the educational values of Internet curricula.[68]

---

[67] *Wall Street Journal*, June 7, 2001, p. 1.
[68] The most aggressive educational corporation is Knowledge Universe, a holding company for a series of education-related companies owned by junk bond financier Michael Milken, who serves as chairman of the company. At the same time, Mr. Milken has established personal philanthropy to educational causes, including those that relate to technology-based learning. One of the company's subsidiaries is called k-12, which is a "complete Internet-based elementary and secondary school being developed by former US Department of Education Secretary William Bennett together with nonprofit partner institutions.

Some companies offer free training to help software developers and other technicians become familiar with their products. Though not originally intended for nonprofit organizations, many companies extend these programs as in-kind donations to nonprofits. Microsoft, locked in a competitive battle with Oracle over market share in the database software niche, gave away $600 million in 1998 in the form of free training, technical support, and marketing for its database, e-mail, and other business systems, according to a report in the *Wall Street Journal*.[69] As a kind of extension of this practice, the company offered $25 million in software and training to an organization called N Power, in an effort to promote the digital conversion of nonprofits. Similarly, Microsoft's community relations program has offered scholarships for the company's certification programs to individuals and to the nonprofit organizations that serve them–for example, the United Negro College Fund.

In addressing the future of web advertising, marketing analysts stress the importance of target marketing, in which advertisers are able to ally themselves with the values of a very specific niche market. "It is increasingly true," say marketing experts David Kenny and John Marshall, "that the companies that can anticipate and meet the real needs of their customers based on where they are located, what they do, and which communities of interest they belong to, will be embraced by consumers as valued partners."[70]

The wisdom of that perspective is indeed well known among dot-coms that market to constituencies that may focus on the needs of the economically disadvantaged. The list of such target markets includes women, ethnic minorities, government institutions, educational institutions, and developing countries. As companies tailor their marketing to each of these categories of customers, they tend to soften their sales pitch with the help of nonprofit partners who can demonstrate how specific products could be useful in serving the public interest.

---

[69] *Wall Street Journal*, August 17, 1998, p. 1.
[70] "Contextual Marketing," by David Kenny and John E. Marshall, *Harvard Business Review*, November-December, 2000, p. 119.

For example, women represent an important consumer group for whom on-line markets tend to emphasize nonprofit tie-ins. iVillage is a company that identified the importance of on-line marketing to women years ago.[71] Its web site has resembled that of a self-help organization created during the women's movement of the 1960s and 1970s. In one of its first acts, iVillage hired a city council representative from Atlanta, named Catherine Woolard, to do grassroots community building, organizing volunteers on behalf of iVillage social projects and introducing the site to women's organizations across the country. The company later pioneered the use of its web site for directing donations to women's organizations, in an approach that later influenced the larger on-line portals. Users were given the opportunity to enter their ZIP Codes to find opportunities for giving and volunteering in their metropolitan areas. The company's marketers also promoted "Women's Giving Circles," in which clusters of women pooled their donations on behalf of women's causes.

The major high-tech company that has gone farthest to integrate nonprofits into its marketing strategy is AOL Time Warner. As a way of extending the old-economy concept of public service advertisements, AOL joined forces with the Benton Foundation to support an initiative called Helping.org. By leveraging the deep market penetration of AOL, it was able to register 650,000 nonprofits in the program by 2002. The database was large enough to enable users to simply input their ZIP Codes to receive a list of volunteer opportunities in their neighborhoods, which are sorted by causes, such as "environment" and "youth."[72] Recently, Helping.org added the service of on-line credit card donations to the same causes, with no transaction fees, and in 2001 began serving as intermediary between givers and receivers. Plans call for the extension of Helping.org internationally where AOL business services are rapidly spreading.

AOL's prominence as an intermediary between contributors and nonprofits explains why smaller dot-coms specializing as

---

[71] www.ivillage.com.
[72] See www.helping.org or www.AOL.com.

intermediaries, such as GreaterGood.com, have gone out of business. Traditional nonprofit intermediaries, such as local United Way agencies, are scrambling to compete.

Creating Customers in Emerging Markets

Perhaps the market most sensitive to the concerns of low-income persons is the government market–not just federal, state and local offices in the United States, but also in developing countries where the government is often the number one customer of transnational corporations. The broadest nonprofit tie-ins to corporate marketing will surely come from market-development efforts earmarked for the developing world. Forrester Research predicts that by 2004, only about a third of on-line commerce will be conducted within the United States. Furthermore, many predict the emergence of a global consumer market by 2010 when as many as four of the world's six billion citizens are expected to access the Internet in their homes or through community locations. The historic effort to build this market will become the focus of market-development activity in most major high-tech companies, as is already the case in a few.[73]

According to Vinod Khosla, noted Silicon Valley venture capitalist of Keiner, Perkins, Caufield & Byers, "Rural services in the developing world will be the fastest growing part of the global economy by 2010."[74] A group of marketing companies that includes Motorola, Hewlett-Packard, Procter & Gamble, and the Ford Motor Company have joined together in a "Bottom of the Pyramid Co-Laboratory" under the leadership of University of North Carolina management guru Stewart Hart to discuss strategies for building tech-based sales in rural villages while offering better opportunities to the poor in those regions.

In an effort to encourage governments to speed up the conversion to "egovernance," many companies have set up business-development units targeting government bureaucrats

---

[73] The first coalition of companies focused on building rural markets in the developing countries emerged under the leadership of Steward Hart of the University of North Carolina. Called the "Bottom of the Pyramid Co-Laboratory," the network included 12 major corporations by mid-2001.

[74] Speech to the World Resources Institute in Seattle, October 16, 2000.

in the developing world. In 1997, IBM became the first to establish an internal research institute, the Institute for Electronic Governance. Its major focus is the production of models for digital approaches to government administration. "Government is at the same place banking was 20 years ago, before they were digitalized and downsized," says Janet Corvo, the former director of the Institute. "By switching to on-line ways of interacting with consumers, the cost of government would plummet, leading to cost savings that could be applied to helping the poor," she said. "At the same time, with the help of electronic networks, the ability of government to uplift the poor could be immensely improved."

With corporations seeking to identify market opportunities in the developing world, a network of nonprofit organizations and initiatives have offered their services as go-betweens for corporate market developers and nonprofits operating in the developing world.[75] Among these organizations, the World Resources Institute (WRI) has taken on the challenge of compiling a data bank of nonprofit/corporate partnerships designed to build markets through IT in the hinterlands of the developing world. WRI has assembled a data bank of business models, conceived by nonprofit organizations. Each of these projects tests ways that technology companies can construct infrastructure, conceive Internet applications, and provide the training necessary to close the digital divide. Says WRI's Allen Hammond, "Companies are searching out nonprofit partners who will help them formulate how to succeed in the far reaches of the globe."[76]

Not everyone believes that nonprofits have the capacity to contribute meaningfully to this market-building effort. "Sure NGOs [non-governmental organizations] are ubiquitous in the developing world. But their problem is that they conduct activities that cannot be scaled up and, for that

---

[75] This list of intermediaries includes Harvard University's Center for International Development within the Kennedy School, the MIT Media Lab ("Digital Nations" program), World Resources Institute, and Digital Partners.

[76] For an update on World Resources Institute's activity in this arena, see www.DigitalDividend.org.

reason, cannot attract investments from the major corporations," said C.K. Prahalad, professor of Business, University of Michigan.[77]

---

[77] See remarks by Dr. Prahalad at www.DigitalDividend.org, which is the web site of the World Resources Institute's Digital Dividends program.

CHAPTER FIVE EXPLORES...

Why high-tech human resources departments ally themselves with the public interest

➤ Morale-building and burnout-prevention strategies involve promoting volunteerism among employees. HR departments are collaborating with nonprofits to encourage social involvement of employees without causing their employees to physically depart from the workplace.

➤ Telementoring, i.e. volunteering via e-mail exchanges, is an important incipient trend.

➤ Employee diversity programs are supporting efforts to extend technology access to African-American and Hispanic populations.

➤ HR departments promote "academies," school-to-work efforts to broaden their base of potential recruits.

➤ Accreditation programs often include scholarships to low-income students.

➤ Since stock options have diminished appeal as a lure for attracting or retaining employees, more companies are appealing to the social values of employees.

Human Resources Management of Digital Companies

The Employee Connection

During the 1980s and 1990s, as stock values in IT companies kept rising, stock options were the magical incentive for high-tech recruiters. Then came the jitters of 2000 and 2001, and suddenly stock options lost value as a way of luring the best and the brightest recruits. Unable to guarantee affluence, corporate human resources (HR) departments were forced to become more creative in identifying non-economic perks to attract and retain their workforce.

That may well be the chief reason why nonprofit organizations are finding willing partners in high-tech human resources departments. Increasingly, a nonprofit such as Catholic Charities or Junior Achievement represents its value to companies not just in terms of "enlightened self-interest" but in tangible terms–as a way of helping the company address a series of workforce problems: low morale/high burnout among employees, shortage of eligible recruits, lack of ethnic diversity, and so on.

Although many employees of digital companies appreciate the high-intensity learning environment, as well as the financial perks,[78] many are dissatisfied with the long hours and the unbalanced lifestyle that lead to early burnout and/or career changes.[79] The average tenure at a digital company is only six years,[80] about half that of other industries. Many HR directors

---

[78] The average wage of high-tech workers is roughly twice that for workers in other industries, see *Wall Street Journal*, June 6, 2001, p. 1.

[79] For a review of the literature on the linkage between employee morale and employee volunteerism, see the Points of Light Foundation web site at www.pointsoflight.org.

[80] This data was quoted from a proprietary report by Microsoft, according to Microsoft's Vice President for Human Resources.

accept the pace as a factor they cannot control. In response, they are searching for ways to win the hearts of employees or, at least, mitigate their stress. Among the techniques being employed: fostering employee interest groups, creating "family friendly" policies, and supporting team-building activities. As these HR teams contemplate strategies in these areas, many contact in-house community relations departments for help.

Building Morale of Employees

Many new internal alliances are being created between corporate morale-builders and corporate "do-gooders." When they meet, the first discussion focuses on a presentation of hard evidence showing employee volunteerism and morale to be closely linked. This convincing data has been gathered for several years by the Points of Light Foundation, a carryover from the first Bush presidency.[81] Concerned that the percentage of employees volunteering in digital companies might be lower than in other industries,[82] some companies have aspired to create "volunteer opportunities" for their employees. "What we are aiming for is to give our employees a chance to draw inspiration from their technical skills," said David Ford, former Director of Community Relations at Lucent Technology.[83]

Thanks to new technologies, employee surveys have become a popular tool for HR strategists to dovetail corporate goals with nonprofit needs. By gathering information regarding employee interests and preferences for community involvement and volunteerism, these surveys yield precious information about how to appeal to the social values of employees. Following a practice pioneered by Levi-Strauss in the mid-1980s, some digital companies used survey information to design programs

---

[81] Points of Light reports that evidence of the link between volunteerism and employee morale is the major factor affecting the increase in corporate volunteerism programs, which are now conducted by 81 percent of the corporations included in the organization's annual survey, compared to 48 percent in 1992. See www.pointsoflight.org.

[82] Some human resources researchers differ on whether volunteerism in IT fields is more or less pervasive than in other fields. Studies of the Community Foundation Silicon Valley foundation have found that, at the very least, the number of volunteerism programs organized formally by corporate management in high-tech firms is on the rise. However, it is unclear whether this data suggests a rise or fall in IT employee volunteerism. See www.siliconvalleygives.org or www.cfsv.org.

[83] Interview in New York, 1999.

to help their employees participate in the community. IBM is perhaps the longest standing practitioner of this approach. For many years, IBM's annual employee survey included questions about their employees' community involvement. As a result, IBM boasts impressive numbers–in 2000, its employees volunteered for a total of 2.8 million hours! One year, IBM sought specific advice from employees on other important topics, such as math education at the K-12 level. "Our employees told us we should be shifting our efforts to the middle-school years," said Stanley Litow, IBM Community Relations Director.

Reinventing Employee Volunteerism

In the mid-1980s, Apple Computer was the first to turn to its technology to establish digital bulletin boards and web sites to link employees to volunteer opportunities. AT&T went further by partnering with the Family Education Company to create a central database to recruit employees and retirees and place them in volunteer positions. More recently, iVillage and AOL Time Warner have taken on the more ambitious tasks of matching entire web-based communities to volunteer opportunities.

Mattel, the toy-maker famous for its Barbie dolls, since the mid-90s has reinvented itself in anticipation of the spread of on-line commerce. The process involved reshaping its employee volunteerism program to embrace the Internet. It established computer learning centers in the schools where employees were already volunteering. The centers were open in the evening, which gave Mattel employees an opportunity to volunteer after hours, and some were even given the chance to volunteer in the same schools their kids attended.

Not all high-tech companies have been content merely to promote volunteerism in the affluent enclaves where most of their employees send their kids to school. The IBM subsidiary Lotus Development Corporation (LDC) has a longstanding policy of giving five paid days annual–leave time for volunteerism–but there is a catch: the perk will only be permitted if the volunteering employees agree to help economically disadvantaged kids.

The LDC example is uncommon. Some of the newer high-tech giants, such as WorldCom, as well as the smaller dot-coms, have rejected the idea of giving employees paid time-off to volunteer for projects that interest them personally–though this practice has been well established in large old-economy companies. The new high-tech trend is toward corporate sponsorship of group volunteer projects in which the same employee workplace teams take time off as a group to embark on "volunteer days." These corporate sponsored activities create more options for the company to gain positive PR as well as boost employee morale.

As with community relations and marketing departments, the category of nonprofits monopolizing the attention of HR departments is public schools. Linking America's classrooms to the Internet has been a huge corporate campaign since 1996, the year that the US Telecom Act of 1996 made wiring schools a national priority. Soon afterward, corporate coalitions sensitive to government pressure emerged to coordinate the activity. NetDay, for example, was vigorously promoted by the Clinton White House.[84] But the granddaddy of such efforts, Cable in the Classroom, was sponsored by a coalition of dozens of cable companies from all facets of the industry who claim to have made in-kind donations of volunteered time valued in the billions of dollars. As a result, it has become known as the most sizable corporate campaign in business history.[85]

Volunteering On-line

Particularly challenging is the effort to promote volunteerism within the workforce without distracting employees from their daily responsibilities. For some companies, the answer to this dilemma is a practice called "telementoring"–a program embraced with great enthusiasm by Hewlett-Packard. "Telementoring" refers to the practice of linking employees by e-mail with those needing help. For example, a Singaporean H-P employee tutor based in Topeka, Kansas, helped a Singaporean sixth grade student of Malay ethnicity develop a web site under

---

[84] www.NetDay.org.
[85] Cable in the Classroom (www.cicon-line.com) is a $2 million-per-week effort, supported by 39 national cable networks and over 8,500 local cable companies, providing schools across the U.S. with free cable hookups and service and (as of 2001) 540 hours per month of commercial-free educational programming available to classrooms with cable connections.

the guidance of her classroom teacher, who was also a participant in the program. The student, who learned about research on the web as well as the mechanics of web development, proudly displayed her web site to demonstrate how her culture has contributed to Singapore's history. The tutor, also of Malay ancestry, was able to share the young girl's pride. Begun in 1998, the program has caught fire within H-P and has been expanded to other companies and other countries through a partnership with a Colorado-based nonprofit organization called the Keystone Center.[86]

How Nonprofits Support High-Tech Diversity

In some high-tech companies, employee volunteerism can help solve another problem that faces HR departments: attracting an ethnically diverse workforce. As digital companies move beyond their traditional base of customers, their employees are mostly Caucasian, or Asian, and are from affluent backgrounds. According to Department of Labor statistics compiled in the 1990s,[87] African-Americans represent just three percent, and Hispanics six percent, of the work force in computer science-related industries, such as computers and telecommunications. These statistics can embarrass these companies, particularly when they are exploited by the media. (In 1998, the *San Francisco Examiner* ran an exposé on the lack of diversity in Silicon Valley, embarrassing local companies and leading to threats of boycotts from advocacy groups, such as the Greenlining Institute. (One group organized a picket line at an Intel convention in San Francisco, chanting, "Intel, Intel. You're not good. We need computers in the 'hood.")

Hoping to preempt such embarrassing news coverage as well as encourage loyalty from the minority employees in their workforce, a number of HR departments have incorporated nonprofit organizations into their diversity strategies. Here are some methods being used:

---

[86] See www.telementor.org.
[87] See www.stats.bls.gov. Studies linking ethnicity to Internet use can be accessed through www.bentonfoundation.org.

- **Helping advocacy groups**. In this field, as in others, IBM has been a pace-setter. Its community relations department (housed within the company's HR unit) brought together national minority organizations whose members include many of Big Blue's own employees. The organizations represented not only ethnic groups, but gays and lesbians as well. They included ASPIRA, Women's Legal Defense Fund, National Urban League, Gay & Lesbian Alliance Against Defamation, LULAC National Education Service Centers, Inc., and the Mexican American Legal Defense and Educational Fund. In each case, the community relations teams met with the staff of each of these organizations offering to create web sites and web-based strategies for the groups. Similarly, the Seattle web company RealNetworks created a subsidiary called WebActive, which creates web sites for advocacy groups, including ethnic groups. AT&T deploys its African-American and Hispanic employees on weekends to provide Internet hook-ups in disadvantaged schools in ethnic neighborhoods.
- **Supporting minority engineering and computer science programs**. For many years, AT&T and Hewlett-Packard have been among the manufacturing companies that have supported the National Action Council for Minorities in Engineering, whose goal is to widen access for minorities to enter computer-related fields. Microsoft has established a broad partnership with the United Negro College Fund to help the organization make the transition to the digital era. In the partnership, faculty and students attend summer programs at Microsoft's Redmond campus to upgrade their computer science skills.
- **Supporting minority suppliers**. It is still uncommon, but a few companies have responded to pressure from internal employee ethnic organizations to increase purchases made from small-business suppliers owned by minorities. In the late 1990s, in a premier effort, Northern Telecom created a $150 million program to locate suppliers within ethnic minority communities in

its service area. Similarly, Sprint worked with a Kansas City community development corporation to establish a "call center" in an African-American neighborhood in Kansas City, quickly creating 200 jobs for low-income residents.

The Biggest HR Challenge: Overcoming the Bottleneck in Recruits

Perhaps the biggest challenge for HR departments of high-tech companies is the need to broaden the base of potential recruits. The need for new high-tech talent has reached crisis proportions. Though Department of Labor (DOL) records show that job growth in the information technology (IT) field is five percent per year, the number of qualified recruits is actually diminishing.[88]

This bottleneck in employment creates two problems for digital companies. First, there is heightened competition to fill job slots. But second, and more pervasive, the shortage of skilled technology professionals slows the process of conversion to digital technologies. Software vendors, value-added resellers, and other technically skilled employees, working independently as consultants or as employees, generate software-based solutions of all kinds. The leading digital companies want to win the loyalty, not just of their own salaried employees but also of contract workers and the broader circle of their "extended families"–software developers, tech support consultants, and independent software venders. Of course, the goal is for these workers to influence clients and others to purchase the company's products. Therein lies another more complicated problem related to the shortage of IT workers that presents a problem for marketing departments in digital companies, as well as for their human resources departments.

Indeed, the shortage is so serious that it transcends the best efforts of HR departments to mitigate the problem. Some companies address the problem by putting together "cross-functional" initiatives, such as Oracle's $50 million commitment

---

[88] See *Business Week*, June 6, 2001.

to help universities in the United States broaden their curriculum in IT-related fields. Other companies and academic institutions have turned with great frustration to their trade associations to address the problem. It has become a frequent topic for such groups as the American Electronics Association. In an unprecedented step, the Silicon Valley political action committee known as TechNet (Technology Network) put the topic on its list of hot-button issues to address with politicians.

Some corporate HR departments have formed partnerships with nonprofits to address the shortage of skilled workers. These efforts include:

- **School-to-Work Programs**. In 1999, IBM brought together executive directors of the leading school-to-work efforts to its Armonk, New York, campus, to consider how to use Big Blue's technology to help IBM recruit skilled workers.
- **Academies**. Cisco Systems is not the only company creating high-tech academies. A cluster of Hollywood studios and other entertainment companies support high school academies and internship programs in new media organized by the Entertainment Industry Development Corporation in Los Angeles.
- **Certification Programs**. 3Com has a sizable program called NetPrep in which high school students train as technicians to service and repair their own schools' computer networks.
- **Community Colleges**. "The number of partnerships linking high-tech companies and community colleges is proliferating wildly," says Edward Pearce, formerly of the American Association of Community Colleges. Computer Associates, for example, has a program that "adopts" community colleges in low-income areas, where it works pro bono while building their staff to capacity.
- **Adult Education/Workforce Development**. Oracle announced a $50 million fund to be spent at universities to find solutions to the IT crisis. IBM established a

signature program on adult education and workforce development to redefine processes for generating jobs for low-income populations.

CHAPTER SIX EXPLORES...

How high-tech lobbyists ally themselves with the public interest

➤ Government affairs strategies of high-tech companies are increasingly focused on "relationship building." For example, they seek to educate and engage government officials, not merely lobby for regulatory relief. They enlist a broad spectrum of nonprofit organizations to support their relationship-building strategies.

➤ In an effort to sell their products and services to government, companies have established internal initiatives, such as IBM's Institute of Electronic Governance, that demonstrate how government functions can be reinvented with the help of technology.

➤ Some nonprofits have been created to support corporate government affairs strategies, often on behalf of low-income communities or public-schools constituencies, for example NetDay and Cable in the Classroom.

➤ Government affairs efforts include researching methods of reducing costs while improving productivity of social services programs.

➤ At local, state, and national levels, corporate officials are serving on task forces organized by influential government officials. In some countries, private sector leaders are providing politicians with leverage to achieve basic reforms in government. In some cases, these task forces have spawned influential public/private partnerships.

➤ Both computer and telecommunications trade associations lobby government agencies for increased funding for education and support for "technology-in-education" programs.

Corporate Government Affairs of Digital Companies

The New High-Tech Corporate Politics

Up until the mid-1990s, the government-affairs strategies of high-tech companies were highly defensive, even by standards of the lawyerly world of corporate lobbyists. Veteran companies, such as AT&T and IBM, filled their Washington, DC, offices with veterans of regulatory warfare. They built relationships with government officials based on a narrowly defined philosophy, catering to the corporation's tactical advantage. Often, the companies were cast unattractively in the media as "black hats" pitted against "white hat" citizen activists arguing for government to intervene on behalf of the poor and excluded. The upstart "new economy" companies, were defensive in a different way–priding themselves on the fact that they were hardly known in Washington and other national capitals around the world. However, among the administration insiders ("policy wonks"), the dot-com companies were known. Government officials were familiar with their disdain for dealings with politicians who threatened to saddle the new-economy companies with onerous regulations. Techno-gurus from the West Coast, such as George Gilder, argued brashly that government should "get out of the way" of the digital entrepreneurs, who they considered to be the economy's heroes.

By the end of the 1990s, however, the entire *political culture* of high-tech firms made an about-face. Now, the high-tech corporations were wearing the white hats. Many of the initiatives already described–wiring schools, delivering distance learning to impoverished rural areas, offering job-training programs via the Internet, and campaigns to close the digital divide in the developing world–all express a trend insiders call "proactive public-affairs."[89] In contrast to the tactical maneuvers deployed by Washington lobbyists in the past, this new trend called for companies to appeal to the public interest in an effort to establish constructive long-term relationships with politicians/ bureaucrats.

In today's high-tech government-affairs office, there is often a fine line between "supporting" government and playing the role of wise tutor, helping bureaucrats get smart about the use of government tools. "Most government officials end up applying the old rules to the new economy without realizing their efforts will be self-defeating," said Link Hoewing, who manages Verizon's Internet-based public affairs strategies from his office in Washington, DC.

Many companies have adopted an almost righteous tone to defend their Internet lobbying practices. "Unless governments set up the right regulatory environment, the entire global effort to close the digital divide will be lost," says Robert Granger, formerly of Hewlett-Packard. "We feel that it is our responsibility as good corporate citizens to press government to establish policies that could use the Internet to uplift the world's poor."

In the case of Verizon, the company has emphasized the importance to society of government investment in "broadband" (high-speed Internet) capabilities in impoverished low-income areas. "If these areas can get high-quality connectivity, efforts to promote learning and entrepreneurship among the poor can accelerate," he said. Mr. Hoewing is not shy about calling upon the company's long-standing relationships with ethnic minority organizations to reinforce the value of broadband. "Way back in 1996 we helped the NAACP get their first web site," he said.

---

[89] Most of the managers who direct government affairs for companies refer to themselves as "public affairs managers" and are housed within "public affairs" departments. Each company has a somewhat different definition for the term "public affairs," but in each case the major activity is to enhance the company's relationship with government officials and politicians as well as to fight for public policies and regulatory changes in their company's interest. Many corporate foundations are located within public affairs departments and, frequently, the director of a company's foundation (or corporate community relations program) reports to a vice-president for public affairs. For perspectives on the profession of public affairs and the government-affairs function of high-tech corporations, see Foundation for Public Affairs, www.pac.org.

"Now the NAACP is helping us get the word out about the importance of passage of broadband legislation."

Using similar rationales, many other telecommunications, computer and media corporations now work through nonprofit organizations to achieve their political aims indirectly and over the long term. Of course, these companies continue to maintain a defensive relationship with government in circumstances when their interests are being directly challenged. But the days of hard-edged, high-tech tactics in the Beltway, in the U.S. state capitals, and in national capitals the world over have come to an end.[90] What caused the change? The dynamics of the digital economy is the subject of so much legislation and regulatory review that many corporate officials now see their role as educating politicians to the new-economy issues and developing Internet-friendly political allies, rather than spending all their energies fighting for this or that legislation. "There are still many public policy hurdles that must be transcended before on-line commerce really takes off," says George Vradenburg, senior vice-president for government affairs at AOL Time Warner. "We have a lot of work to do to help government officials to be able to see the alignment between their interests and ours."

In fact, Mr. Vradenburg himself is considered by his peers in the high-tech industry a primary architect of the shift toward a "kinder, gentler" public affairs strategy. At a time when Microsoft was locked in a bitter dispute with the Department of Justice, Mr. Vradenburg encouraged the White House to put the digital divide issue "front and center" at the G-8 Summit in Okinawa, Japan, in 2000. The summit then became a showcase for American public/private initiatives focused on the use of the Internet for public benefit. Insiders in the government-affairs field saw this as a wise move, and soon every major company felt pressured to match (or build upon) its competitor's social initiatives.

---

[90] Considered the most prominent exponent of lobbying practices of high-tech companies, David Hart, a professor at the Harvard University Kennedy School of Government's Center for Business and Government, has a number of publications that address the transformation and broadening of the political strategies of technology companies. See *New Economy, Old Economy: The Evolving Role of the High-tech Industry in US Politics*, Brookings Institution, 2001. For references to this and other publications, see http://ksghome.harvard.edu/~.DHart.CSIA.Ksg/research.html.

Here are some reasons why the companies are moving toward more "proactive" relations with government.

The Internet

Increasingly, the U.S. Congress and its counterparts in other countries address a plethora of legislative proposals directly or indirectly related to the Internet–taxation of ecommerce, R&D tax credits, intellectual property issues, special visas for professional employees. As the companies refashion their own strategies around the Internet, they find that government often holds the cards. After all, the Internet is greatly influenced by government policy and government-funded research in universities. In order to convey their point of view toward such issues as taxation of on-line commerce, companies feel they must build positive relationships with legislators and bureaucrats.

Fear of Regulation

The Telecommunications Act of 1996 was poorly received by some telecom companies because it is believed to impose hidden taxes on major telecom providers. Some now see an opportunity to shape the thinking of lawmakers and bureaucrats to include their point of view in any further regulation, particularly on behalf of "universal service" at federal and state levels.

Sales

Some leading companies, such as Oracle, claim that government is now their top customer. As companies emphasize sales outside the United States, where governments represent a larger share of the potential market, relations with the U.S. government has even greater strategic importance. Harvard University's Jerry Mechling says that the digitalization of federal, state, and local bureaucracies has just begun and may have been accelerated by the 2001 downturn in the economy. Through high-tech corporate initiatives, companies have shown the government how they can save time and money in administrative functions, such as education or social services, by converting to the tools of digital technology Noting that government is its "top customer," Oracle joined with its CEO Larry Ellison to announce a $50 million program to offer networked computers and mentorships in the nation's public schools.

Cross-Industry Coalitions

The convergence of telecommunications, computer, and media industries has resulted in broad public affairs alliances, such as the Information Technology Industry Council,[91] which often conducts its own PR-related educational activities. "Leading companies in all three industries have joined forces to encourage Washington officials to see the "upside potential of the Internet," says Charles Firestone, who heads Aspen Institute's Communications and Society program. These broad coalitions make possible public service campaigns such as "NetDay" in wiring schools to the Internet.

These trends toward proactive relations represent a shift to a more sophisticated, complicated strategy in which companies appeal to the general public via mass media while targeting government leaders (to achieve public policy goals) through sponsored events. An indirect "soft" approach to government affairs is hardly new or unique to digital companies. For more than a decade, Fortune 500 companies have been taking an indirect approach to government affairs, according to the Public Affairs Council, an association of government affairs executives. "Despite the common perception that corporate government affairs is a matter of lobbying, [digital companies'] Washington strategies have broadened in recent years to include a cluster of techniques," says Leslie Rosensweig, of the Foundation for Public Affairs. "Corporate public affairs professionals are becoming more reliant on 'soft' tactics, like public relations and philanthropy." She added, "…when a company gains a reputation for promoting good works, it creates a more trusting and nuanced dialogue over issues that might divide them with government officials."[92]

---

[91] See www.itic.org.
[92] Telephone interview, 2000. See www.pac.org.

Internationalization

Each year, the major high-tech companies in the advanced economies gain an increasing share of their total profits from overseas operations. For example, Verizon, which was known as a regional U.S. telecom a few years ago, had operations in 40 countries by 2002. As these companies establish themselves as global powerhouses, more of their activity becomes concentrated in fostering Internet-friendly policies in Europe, Japan, and the emerging markets. The situation has spawned several international corporate coalitions whose seminars and networking sessions press the case for market-based and "pro-competition" approaches to public policy.[93] To justify such policies without seeming to be self-serving, they frame international strategies in ways that stress the public interest.

The shift in high-tech public affairs strategies has led to a broadening and deepening of public affairs strategies in which nonprofit organizations are playing important roles.

Perhaps the most dramatic change can be found in the political action committees in the industry. The largest and most well-known of them, TECHNET, Silicon Valley's technology network,[94] astonished its peers across corporate America by putting "education reform" ahead of the conventional issues of concern to corporate lobbyists, such as tax relief. (In 2001, TECHNET put at the top of its list the passage of a "Technology Talent Bill," increasing the number of science, math, and technology graduates from American educational institutions.) In fact, the political action committee has made the shortage of information technology workers a national *cause celebre* and has aggressively campaigned for companies to establish strategies to tackle the problem. TECHNET's campaign to digitalize schools has been considered the most powerful corporate lobbying initiative for school reform, especially in California. While turning its back on corporate antagonism to new taxation, the lobbying group has argued passionately–and successfully–for increased funding of education.

---

[93] The two most prominent global corporate coalitions both emanated from Washington, DC. They are the Global Internet Infrastructure Commission (www.giic.org) and the Global Business Dialogue on Ecommerce (www.gbde.org).

[94] See www.technet.org.

Rather than stay clear of government, thousands of high-tech executives around the world have eagerly volunteered to serve on government task forces. The effect has turned high-tech moguls into celebrities. A good example is in India where Narawana Murthy, CEO of Bangalore's oldest and most successful software company, Infosys, has become Prime Minister Atal Behari Vajpayee's chief IT advisor. Mr. Murthy's views are sought out by the media as much as those of any government minister. He is not the only one who gets such treatment in India. "Every time I go to India, I'm swarmed by autograph seekers as if I were a pop star," said Kanval Rekhi, a prominent Indian venture capitalist based in Silicon Valley who now advises the Indian government on methods of promoting social entrepreneurship.

Aware of the new mood of high-tech social activism, many nonprofit think tanks have offered themselves as partners with companies that want to align with respectable public policymakers. The flagship think tanks in Washington–for example the Center for Strategic and International Studies, Cato Institute, and American Enterprise Institute–have all tacked IT initiatives onto their organizational charts and signed on high-tech firms as annual supporters. Dozens of universities nationwide also have high-tech public policy programs that respond to corporate benefactors. For example, Cisco Systems supported a research program at University of Texas in Austin pinpointing how the Internet economy contributes to America's economic development.

Apart from established think tanks, another class of think tanks have emerged to give voice to high-tech corporate view on business and social issues linked to the Internet. The most successful is the Center for Democracy and Technology, led by Jerry Berman, broadly supported by top high-tech companies. More recently, the corporate-friendly Internet Policy Institute emerged from Berman's leadership. (A recent IPI report revealed the results of a Yankelovich poll showing that a large portion of Americans, 50 percent, "think the private sector is best equipped to set policies for the Internet."[95])

---

[95] See Internetpolicy.org. See press release for Sept. 6, 2000.

One of the most aggressively pro-corporate nonprofit think tanks was the now-defunct United States Internet Council. In just two years, USIC identified lawmakers at both the state and national level who were predisposed to forming cooperative relations with Internet-based companies. It also organized "Internet caucuses" among government officials. "These officials are growing into a critical mass in many states [and] are inclined to sit down with the companies and find common ground," said Milton Rhodes, legislative liaison for USIC. In fact, some political insiders credited the organization with the successful establishment of a moratorium on taxation of on-line commerce. More recently, a think tank that has become broadly embraced by the telecommunications corporations in the United States is Citizens for Sane Economies, which encourages governments' conversion to Internet-based approaches to public policies.

Another "soft" strategy used by corporate government affairs offices is sponsorships. A popular approach is the training of government officials, such as the governments' own information officers. A related tactic: awarding grants to nonprofit reward programs that honor government officials for their wise use of technology. The computer hardware company Gateway sponsors an awards program that recognizes government agencies for their effective use of web sites for innovative solutions in delivering government services. (A recent winner: the state of Florida.)

Some companies have established think tanks of their own that challenge government bureaus to reinvent themselves with the latest digital tools. Rather than follow the pattern of outsourcing research, IBM has created its own Washington, D.C-based IBM Institute for Electronic Governance, addressing the link between on-line technology and traditional government issues, such as citizen participation and trust in government. "We present the best practices in government's use of technology," said Janet Caldow, the institute's director.

The institute's web site in 2001 included an assessment of ways for K-12 schools to reap gains in productivity through digitalization.[96]

---

[96] See www.ieg.ibm.com.

The K-12 education issue is a common denominator of all the new high-tech corporate strategies. Taking a leadership role in public education reform not only plays well to employees, community leaders, and in-house marketers, it also is viewed favorably by government officials at many levels. Aware of the regulators' scrutinizing eye, many companies put a distinctively political spin on the situation. For example, Sun Microsystems went to the Clinton White House for support of its NetDay initiative for wiring schools. During the Clinton era, Cisco Systems responded to a federal effort to make enterprise zones as a magnet for jobs in the IT sector. Cisco promised to put one of its Networking Academy Programs in "a high school in every empowerment zone." Similar initiatives include IBM's Education Reform Summit and America Online's (AOL) summit on making the Internet safe for children.

Support for NetDay and Other Cross-Industry Alliances

Support for NetDay was linked to government affairs strategies. Inspired by Sun Microsystem's John Gage, and quickly embraced by President Clinton and Vice President Al Gore, the corporate public affairs offices often became advocates for their companies' embrace of the initiative.

Local Public/Private Partnerships

Despite all the activity from multinational corporations, according to United States Internet Council president Bill Myers, "the most enduring and sustained approach to public/ private partnerships is occurring at the local level." Perhaps the most high-profile initiative is the Joint Venture: Silicon Valley, a San-Jose-based effort to "create a neutral space between government and business." In Seattle, William Gates, Sr., (father of Microsoft's CEO) serves as chair of the Technology Alliance, a coalition of business and government leaders in the State of Washington, aiming to develop high-speed networks and other technology innovations for the state's schools.

How high-tech R&D departments ally themselves with the public interest

➤ Hi-tech budgets tripled in size in the 1990s, and their chief technology officers became tech superstars, some of whom have worked behind the scenes influencing the direction of their companies' social initiatives.

➤ Many high-tech research departments are looking beyond traditional ties with academic engineering departments, sponsoring interdisciplinary programs within universities focusing on the social impacts of their technology.

➤ Corporate researchers are "beta testing" their products and services in the public schools and in community-based nonprofit organizations. In some cases, these experiments have affected the commercial strategies of high-tech firms.

➤ High-tech research is undergoing rapid globalization, and many corporations have established research units in emerging markets. These overseas research outposts are responding to government customers by adapting their companies' products and services to the needs of the developing world. Some have established their own ties to academic laboratories and community-based non-profit organizations within developing countries.

➤ Experiments conducted by corporate R&D departments may contribute to a fundamental shift in corporate strategy as these companies seek business models that allow them to shift from a "product focus" to a "service focus," for example, allowing customers to order software services over the Internet rather than upgrading their own software. Some companies believe that community-based NGOs are ideal settings to explore radically new ways to service customers in this way.

Research and Development

Beta Testing Among Nonprofits

Just as they have found a foothold within other corporate departments, nonprofits have made inroads into research laboratories of high-tech corporations. As a result, some corporate research and development (R&D) divisions are doing what Harvard Business School management guru Rosabeth Moss Kanter calls "beta testing in the social sector."[97] No longer outsourcing research to universities alone, R&D departments are testing innovations in community settings. Increasingly, corporate research programs are being outsourced in unconventional places: in Philadelphia's inner-city public schools, Senagal's NGOs, and in India's academic labs, where handheld devices are being adapted to the economic needs of illiterate adults.

One shouldn't overemphasize the scale of the trend. Of the companies interviewed for this report, only a few have embraced this practice. Still, the early signs of R&D/nonprofit connection, occurring at a time of corporate retrenchment, have to be regarded as very good news–both for the beleaguered industry itself and for the nonprofits seeking corporate partners willing to stick with them for the long haul. Though corporate research departments elsewhere in America have not traditionally played an important role in the social initiatives of corporations,[98] a number of trends suggest that this may be changing, at least in

---

[97] "From Spare Change to Real Change," by Rosabeth Moss Kander, *Harvard Business Review*, May-June 1999, pp. 123-131.

[98] In the annual surveys of community relations managers conducted by the Center for Corporate Citizenship at Boston College, these managers have never rated research departments high on their list of "internal customers" who are served by a company's giving program. See www.bc.edu/aup/csom/ccc.

the Internet industries. Some of the largest and most significant signature initiatives (especially H-P's e-Inclusion and IBM's Reinventing Education) contain the stamp of in-house research departments.

Perhaps more significantly, many of the industry's R&D superstars have been vociferous behind-the-scenes advocates, encouraging their companies to take a strong stance on social issues.

It is difficult to over-estimate the degree to which the core values of the Internet industries are represented by its "head geeks," whose prestige often transcends that of the chief executive officers in their corporations. That "pride-in-geekdom" may well explain why Bill Gates, in 1999, gave up the chief executive's slot in arguably the most successful corporation in history to assume the seemingly modest title of "Chief Software Architect." His reasoning? "It means I can turn great ideas into innovative solutions,"[99] The word "solutions" is the key here. Many of the industry's top researchers are intent on grappling with technological solutions to some of society's most vexing problems. This may explain why these researchers have been willing to leave the confines of their laboratories for "real-world" circumstances in the community where the value of their ideas can be tested.

Chief Researchers as Social Activists

The researcher who best personifies the values of the socially engaged engineer is Vinton Cerf. Like Mr. Gates, he holds a rather nerdy title: "Senior Vice President of Internet Architecture" at WorldCom, where he is better known than CEO Bernard Ebbers (whose expertise is thought to lie *merely* in the business realm). Dr. Cerf is the "engineer's engineer," a scientist who in the early phase of his career created a crucial phase of the TCP/IP communication protocol leading to the creation of the Internet. Cerf is nowadays regarded as a kind of Internet icon and a high-profile spokesman for the Internet's role as a benevolent resource for the planet.

---

[99] See www.microsoft/billgates.

Many of Cerf's views about the possibilities of the Internet's role in society have been expressed over the years in the Internet Society, an organization he helped to create. The Society is a holding company for a network of nonprofits that define the evolution of the Internet. He was its president from 1992 until 1995. During that period, a main concern was whether the Internet would remain robust as it became ubiquitous and brought cascading change in its wake. It was important to Cerf that the Internet not be captured by proprietary interests or technical factors that limit its universal access. Rather than assume that access would take care of itself, Cerf remarked famously, "The Internet is for everyone–but it won't be unless WE make it so."[100] He later established a division within the Internet Society to take on social issues, called the "Internet Societal Needs Task Force."[101] Among its projects, an effort to explore web-based solutions for physical impairments, including his own: Cerf suffers from a hearing impairment.

In the year 2000, Cerf put his reputation on the line when he was tapped by the Clinton administration to chair a crucial White House meeting. The topic was the digital divide. The challenge was to present a united front between public and private sectors, which would ultimately lead to the adding, by the United States, of the digital divide to the action agenda for the upcoming G-8 meeting in Okinawa. At the time, many in the private sector had not yet recovered from regulatory warfare from the Telecommunications Act of 1996, which left the door open for further regulation regarding how universal access for the poor would be funded. "Vint was the only one respected by all parties to get people to the table and to get people to agree. We ended up with a market-based framework which set the right tone for the G-8 who embraced the concept," said Denis Gilhooly, of the United Nations Development Programme, one of the meeting's organizers.[102] Besides serving externally as a leader in the movement to close the digital divide, Cerf is among

---

[100] Vinton Cerf speech to the Internet Society, April 7, 1999.
[101] Technology-based approaches to special needs is one of the themes of the Internet Society Task Force, a division of the Internet Society, in which Vint Cerf has played a leading role. See www.istf.org.
[102] Interview in New York City, 2000.

the executives serving on the board of the WorldCom Foundation. He has also been an advisor to WorldCom itself in its own response to the digital divide, expressed in a schools-based initiative called "Marco Polo."

Despite Cerf's leadership, there is no evidence that WorldCom's research agenda has been influenced by Cerf's attention to social issues. To find synergy between tech superstars and the research agenda of companies, one has to go to Silicon Valley–where corporate strategy and politics are closely interwoven. Among the standouts is Sun Microsystems–and two of its strongest research personalities: Chief Scientist Bill Joy and Chief Researcher John Gage.

Having been an innovator on the UNIX system as a young graduate student at University of California, Berkeley, Bill Joy spearheaded Sun's "open systems" philosophy as its top cheerleader. Just as "open society" has taken on almost theological overtones in the world of philanthropy, "open systems" causes goose-bumps in the Silicon Valley's digerati who have been fiercely opposed to Microsoft's more proprietary approach to software. Gleeful at the industry's embrace of "distributed computing technology," Joy is also articulate in explaining how the open approach serves society's interests–and how a proprietary approach does not. In particular, he emphasizes how the Internet's open approach enables collaboration needed by society. In 2001 he authored the latest version of the distributed-computing approach, called "Community Source Licensing Model," which "facilitates cooperation with educators, customers, researchers and other partners."[103]

As the anti-globalization movement caused many nonprofit networks to close ranks in opposition to the dominant IT corporations,[104] Joy managed to retain his activist pedigree. He won over corporate naysayers by beating them at their own game. In an April 2000 *Wired* cover story called, "Why the

---

[103] Further information on Community Source Licensing is available at www.sun.com/jini.
[104] A good information source for these networks is an on-line magazine called *Community Technology Review* (comtechreview.org), based at the University of Massachusetts-Boston, College of Public and Community Service. For Computer Professionals for Social Responsibility, see www.cpsr.org. See also Community Technology Network, www.ctcnet.org.

Future Doesn't Need Us," he turned his back on the positive stories about "digital opportunities"[105] to present a dark view of the inherent dangers of freedom presented by the upcoming era of robotics, nanotechnologies, and genetics, which he says will define the corporate-dominated future. The article led to his appearance in conferences of progressive organizations like the "Computer Professionals for Social Responsibility" and "The Association for Community Technology." Not limited to critiques, many of these discussions have evolved into pragmatic discussions about tapping open-source software to solve social problems–and working toward a future other than the one Joy depicted in his article.

In 1998, Joy, still looking very much the fresh-faced graduate student, was given a platform to express his views regarding the social impact of computing, as co-chair of the most prestigious White House venue for deliberating the evolution of the Internet. Called the Presidential Information Technology Advisory Committee, it is composed equally of computer science deans from the top universities and Joy's colleagues in the corporate world. Though the committee was formed in the Clinton era, it was quickly extended by executive order as soon as President George W. Bush took office in early 2001.[106] Though the advisory group was originally intended for the narrow purpose of defining the federal role in researching the next-generation Internet, it caused a stir in industry circles because it argued that the public should not fund the Internet's *technological* evolution without a parallel exploration of the Internet's *social* impact. The result: Congress earmarked $150 million for the National Science Foundation to spend at universities and other nonprofits wanting to scrutinize the plusses and minuses of society's digitalization.

Another of Sun's technological gurus who has taken an even greater stance towards social action is John Gage. He retained

---

[105] The theme is best expressed in the Digital Opportunities Task Force in which a global coalition of nonprofit organizations, corporations, governments and inter-governmental agencies assess ways to bring "digital opportunities" to the non-affluent. See www.dotforce.org.
[106] Congress has extended the mandate of the Advisory Community until June 2003. Since its initial report, the Committee has produced several reports that address the digitalization of libraries, schools, and the issue of the digital divide itself. See www.itrd.gov/ac.

the title of Sun's chief researcher[107] even after wandering into the realms of public policy as a recent Visiting Fellow at Harvard University's Kennedy School of Government. In 1996, at a time when World Wide Web pages were still being used for organizational brochures, Mr. Gage became convinced that the web could be used as a self-organizing tool for conceiving, implementing, and evaluating social projects on a massive scale. With the full backing of his company, Mr. Gage put together a dazzling web site that created "NetDay" in 1996. It was a volunteer project conducted almost entirely through its web site. Since the onset of the project, 500,000 volunteers have wired over 50,000 schools and libraries to the Internet, he says. Begun in the United States, NetDays had been held in thirty-five countries by 2001.[108]

But if NetDay expressed the possibilities of leveraging the Internet for social purposes, it still did not engage the Sun research department itself on social projects. But that may change. In 2000 the company's researchers announced a "Digital Journey" initiative. The company describes it as an effort to "understand how technologies affect social and cultural contexts."

H-P Labs Seeks To Reinvent H-P

Among those interviewed for this publication, the corporate research department that has been most explicit about aligning its strategies with the public interest is H-P Labs, the venerable R&D division of Hewlett-Packard. H-P Labs stands out for putting social issues at the center of its *overall* strategy for bringing innovation into the company. From the outset, Lab scientists have had a starring role in the World e-Inclusion[109] program. "The seeds of e-Inclusion were planned in the labs," said James Sheats, a laboratory scientist who was one of the originators of the initiative. As of 2000, he was one of 20 professionals within H-P assigned full time to the initiative.

---

[107] Gage's personal web site is a technological marvel. It even allows viewers to check to see if he is speaking on a given date and request a booking. All without making a phone call! See www.johngage.com.
[108] www.johngage.com.
[109] See earlier reference, p. 6.

Explaining why a corporate lab would embrace a social change project, Sheats says that the initiatives fit well into H-P Labs culture, which has had a leadership role not matched by labs in other companies. "In the late 1980s, many companies broke up their research departments so that they became focused on product divisions (like Eastman Kodak's color lab), and many of them were given only a six- to nine-month timeframe. It was an attempt to emulate the Japanese who were better at transferring technologies to the market. The focus is always 'what's our next product.' H-P Labs didn't go in that direction, since we were already good at transferring technologies. Although we also have short-term development efforts linked to divisions, we have been supported to think three to five years out."[110]

With the long leash given to the H-P Labs and its mandate to think out of the box, scientists at the Labs have had the luxury to explore approaches running counter to the dominant culture of the company–such as how to move the H-P printer business toward a more environmentally sustainable approach. This explains how e-Inclusion is in tune with the zealous environmentalist values of many of H-P Lab scientists. Sheats conveyed the views of Stewart Hart, a University of North Carolina management professor, who apparently played an important role in the thinking about economic development that underlies e-Inclusion's strategy.[111]

As interpreted by Sheats, Hart's thesis is that using technology to make people more affluent ...will add stress to the environment. "The more affluent you are, the more you consume the earth's resources." says Sheats. Therefore, he says, if you wipe out poverty in the bottom 80 percent, imitating the pattern of the past, you increase the strain on the earth's environment by five times....One way around this problem is by developing environmentally sustainable technology that allows people to become more affluent without damaging the environment. "That epitomizes our challenge here at H-P Labs,"

---

[110] Interview in Palo Alto, California, 2001.
[111] For a framework that links corporate strategy to environmental sustainability, see Stewart Hart's "Beyond Greening," in *Harvard Business Review*, January-February, 1997.

said Sheats. "We're interested here to find affordable ways to transform H-P's products and services so that they are sustainable–environmentally and commercially."

When asked how this relates to H-P's business model, Stewart said that e-Inclusion represents an opportunity for H-P to marry Hart's environmental sustainability ideas to the thinking about the development of sustainable businesses when the world approaches Internet ubiquity, giving access to four billion consumers who have been beyond the reach of global capitalism. "Those who look at the business models that will become viable in the next generation of computing see a trend pointing toward services, not products." H-P may now be known as the maker of reliable products. But in the future our success depends on whether we can deliver services better than our competitors, whether we can *empower* them. It all depends on finding out what they need that can be delivered with the help of technology."

This view is not just H-P's alone. The shift from products to services is, by some accounts, the dominant theme of all hardware companies in the past several years. Its underlying premise is that computing companies must scramble to reorient their business models to offer technologies as services provided (by customer demand) over the Internet rather than requiring customers to maintain their own hardware and software. "Microsoft calls it 'dot-net,' Oracle calls it 'network services,' and Sun calls it 'Open Network Environment.' But they are all talking about a radical shift towards revamping their technologies as services offered over the web," said authors John Hegel III and John Seely Brown in an article in *Harvard Business Review*.[112]

To Sheats, e-Inclusion is not merely a way to reduce world poverty in an environmentally friendly way. It presents the means–perhaps even H-P's most important means–to become a corporate powerhouse, capable of beaming services five billion consumers who are not yet on-line. E-Inclusion is not the first example of H-P's attempt to strengthen its role as a service company. While its competitor, IBM's profitable consulting

---

[112] *Harvard Business Review*, October, 2001, p. 105.

division, was leading Big Blue into the services era, H-P tried to acquire the consulting firm PricewaterhouseCoopers LLP for $16 billion in 2000, in one of Carly Fiorina's first acts as CEO. Following that debacle, Ms Fiorina, in close interaction with H-P Lab staff, became convinced that e-Inclusion would present a way of showcasing H-P's intellectual capital and symbolizing H-P's overhaul as a company–now dedicated to serving the diverse needs of the traditional non-English speaking world–those who live beyond the confines of homogenized modern culture.

Ms. Fiorina decided that the vast expanse of the non-affluent in the developing world–virgin territory from H-P's point of view–should be considered a huge testing ground for services delivered over the Internet. "In effect, she told us here at H-P Labs to release our creative energies, by going directly to the settings where problems of poverty exist. We quickly looked for nonprofit partners who could give us that insight," said H-P's Robert Granger, one of the managers of e-Inclusion.[113]

By 1999, H-P Labs scientists had attended enough conferences on the topic of the digital divide to know that the field of international development was full of anticipation about new "sustainable business models" that could be employed by IT-informed entrepreneurs working in the world's villages.[114] Sheats felt that the time was right for a major IT company to see whether this new approach could be scaled up as the Internet reaches the emerging markets. "Middlemen give farmers just 60 cents a pound for their coffee while customers in advanced countries buy it for $15 a pound," he said. "The sort of problem we want to solve is whether we can intervene with Internet kiosks in villages to find ways of greatly increasing the share that goes to the farmer. If we can do that and find a way of delivering services over the Internet to allow the farmer and his agricultural cooperatives to get a better and better share over time, we are sure to find new ways that businesses delivering these services can make money."

[113] Interview in Palo Alto, California, 2001.
[114] For an update on this trend, see "Survey of Technology and Development" the *Economist*, November 10, 2001, pp. 3-14.

Within a year of that conversation, e-Inclusion did find a number of testing sites for such projects, distributed in community-based settings around the world. In Senegal, it was Internet connectivity and training involving a partnership with the Peace Corps; in Costa Rica it was working with an NGO to develop handheld devices to help farmers streamline production; in Ghana, an Internet development center; in Brazil an e-commerce rural tie-in with McDonald's restaurants, and in India, handheld devices were used in sugarcane production. Perhaps most importantly, H-P Labs expanded its own research infrastructure to reflect the company's emphasis on solving social problems. In October 2001, the company inaugurated a new research lab in India, focused on finding IT innovations relevant to the particular needs of emerging economies. "We want to link our technology to the social, economic, and technological drivers of change in the developing world," said the lab's new director, Dr. Srinwasan Ramani.[115]

Education plus Globalization Equals R&D Breakthroughs

As noted earlier, Harvard Business School management guru Rosabeth Moss Kanter feels that, increasingly, corporate research departments are turning to community based nonprofits to "set up learning laboratories, extend their capabilities, get feedback from early users about product potential and gain experience working with underserved and emerging markets."[116] Certainly, H-P Labs philosophy is consistent with this view. Kanter, in her 1999 *Harvard Business Review* article said that, after years of dismissing "the social sector" as irrelevant to research departments, companies were beginning to see their involvement with nonprofits as a vital source of *innovation.*"[117] She predicted that more companies would see the wisdom of conducting experiments in the community in order to gain a leg up on their competitors. Two long-term trends that confirm

---

[115] H-P news release, October 9, 2001. See www.hp.com.
[116] "From Spare Change to Real Change," Rosabeth Moss Kanter, *Harvard Business Review*, May-June, 1999.
[117] Kanter, op cit, pp. 123-131.

the deepening role of nonprofits, as Moss Kanter advocates, are, first of all, the trend toward the *outsourcing* of R&D activities, particularly regarding the burgeoning field of educational research. The second trend is the *globalization* of research and development, where companies are being forced to consider how their products and services can connect to governments of emerging markets.

A Distributed Approach to Corporate R&D

A year 2000 survey of R&D by members of the Industrial Research Institute underscored the long-term trend: "R&D is more internally and externally collaborative," says a recent report summarizing the responses of 235 chief technology officers who are members of the Industrial Research Institute.[118] The report concludes, "Every year there is a larger percentage of corporate research being outsourced to universities, institutes, research consortia and nonprofit organizations."

One reason R&D is becoming so distributed within and without the corporation is the ever-increasing amount of research available. The typical corporate R&D department tripled its budget between 1987 and 1997, according to the Industrial Research Institute. Microsoft Research's budget alone reached $4 billion in 2000. Even while laying off thousands of employees amid the dot-com bust of 2001, some corporations publicly declared their intention *not* to cut back their search for lab-inspired innovations.[119]

Educational institutions have become one of the most valuable conduits through which research departments have seen the value of collaboration with nonprofits. Since the mid-1990s, as companies began to reinvent their strategies around the Internet, they redoubled their ties with academic researchers where much of the technical expertise on the Internet is concentrated. More than half of high-tech industry patents in the 1990s credited some form of university research, according to CHI Research, Inc.[120]

---

[118] Quotation is from www.iriinc.org/web/.
[119] For a discussion about the logic of expanding R&D during a downturn, see *Wall Street Journal*, May 22, 2001. www.wsj.com.
[120] Cited by *Business Week*, August 31, 1998, p. 94.

Universities, for their part, have aggressively promoted their own ties with corporations. In a practice pioneered by Stanford University and the Massachusetts Institute of Technology, licensing deals are now common in hundreds of universities, which are the outgrowths of these corporate/nonprofit partnerships. Throughout the 1990s, many of these corporate/ academic partnerships began to focus on a broader set of research questions involving interdisciplinary programs in universities– the public schools, libraries, and community organizations.

In 1991, Bell Atlantic, in its "Project Explore," created one of the first efforts to develop computer networks for public schools. Part of the effort involved giving computers to 135 inner city students and their teachers to use at home.[121] The effort, which was soon adopted in various forms by research units of many other high-tech corporations, proved to provide crucial information that was later adapted as educational software offered to public schools. Microsoft engaged researchers to track how the learning of low-income kids changes when they use laptop computers. When IBM created its "Reinventing Education" initiative, the effort involved creating tools to connect parents to teachers digitally so that parents could view their children's school work at home or at a community center. In Philadelphia, IBM researchers' participation in a school program, created by Big Blue's community relations department, led to new voice recognition software, tailored to the distinct voices of students of different ages and ethnic groups.[122]

R&D's Globalization

Corporations based outside the United States have steadily increased their U.S.-based research facilities to gain proximity to the explosive regions that have served as the foundation for IT innovation. Less well-known is the flip side of the globalization of research: According to a 2000 report by the Industrial Research Institute, over 100 U.S.-based multinationals have acquired laboratories abroad, many of them lured into cyberparks in places like Hydrabad, India, Taipei, Taiwan and Tel Aviv, Israel.

---

[121] Moss Kanter, *HBR*, May-June, 1999, p. 124.
[122] Interview with Robin Wilner, IBM headquarters, 1999.

The first generation of these remote research facilities continued to work on solutions that served needs of high-end customers in more advanced countries. But IBM researchers were the first to adapt its overseas research agendas to meet overseas needs. As early as 1998, its New Delhi-based scientists had joined with the Indian government to explore how voice recognition software could revitalize India's literacy strategies. Though few commercial R&D facilities have joined H-P's efforts to explicitly find the link between their business strategies and the needs of the poor, this overseas research infrastructure may well find the needed solutions. Geoffrey Kirkman, who heads the Information Technologies Group of Harvard University's Center for International Development, has looked at the laboratory advances that serve the needs of the world's poor in his 2001 report, "Out of the Lab and Into the Development World."[123] He notes that many of the core themes of concern to basic researchers in the IT field address the need to become relevant to the problems vexing the developing world, such as the need to drastically reduce the cost of computing for the poor, or to produce on-line services that are accessible to community groupings of people who use cybercafes or Internet kiosks, rather than focusing on individual consumers who own their own personal electronic devices.

As noted by Kirkman, academic laboratories, rather than their corporate counterparts, are in a better position to take the lead on digital divide-related activities. "It is still true that companies do not perceive the latent demand for the Internet in the developing world; thus technology is not produced with the cost and design constraints of developing countries," he said. "We may find that university researchers will be leading their corporate partners into this field," he said.[124]

MIT Media Labs offers a good example of how academic research laboratories are luring their corporate partners into the digital divide space. On the campus of the Massachusetts

---

[123] "Out of the Labs and Into the Developing World: Using Appropriate Technologies to Promote Truly Global Internet Diffusion," by Geoffrey Kirkman, *Journal of Human Development*, Vol.2, No.2, 2001.
[124] Interview in Cambridge, Mass., 2001.

Institute of Technology, the Media Lab since 1996 has promoted the idea that the digital future lay in the convergence of all media, leading to applications beyond anyone's imagination. The Lab's creative process in exploring these multimedia advances coincided nicely with the corporate world's eagerness for developing new markets using the latest technological innovations. Soon, the Media Lab became the most successful of all academic labs in gaining a long and loyal list of corporate supporters. The brainchild of an academic entrepreneur named Nicholas Negroponte, the Media Lab in many ways adopted the format for the standard "corporate affiliates" programs that are common in university engineering departments: corporate labs pay an annual fee for a chance with academics who are working on the very frontiers of science. But under Negroponte's leadership the Lab was a kind of cultural event. One of the founders of *Wired* magazine, his column on the back page of that magazine defined trends in the hip world, and the Media Lab established a kind of balance between hip and academic.

In the late 1990s, some critics of the Lab accused it of venturing toward the self-absorbed realm of "yuppies." All indications were that the Lab's future lay in an examination of the inner world–cutting edge explorations into perception, the nature of creativity, artificial reality, and the use of "intelligent agents" to do the bidding of the consumer. Some poked fun at the Lab's embrace of "wearable computers" and "smart clothing," which were displayed by glamorous models walking down Milan runways. The Lab seemed to make no apology for mixing the frivolous with the meaningful.

But in 1999 a change occurred. Under the leadership of the Media Lab's academic director, Sandy Pentland, and an influential faculty member, Mitch Resnick, the Lab led an effort to extend the Lab toward the social sector, not just in the United States but in poor countries as well. Recognizing that much of the future of computing lay beyond the saturated, high-end markets of the developed world, Pentland and Resnick co-founded MIT's "Digital Nations Consortium." The idea was to enlist entire countries as members in the same way the Lab had recruited corporations. Just as the Lab offered companies a chance to find a path into new technology to serve their customers, the Digital Nations concept was not to impose solutions but to "empower peoples from all walks of life to develop their own solutions." The kick-off event of the Consortium, held in July of 2001, attracted representatives of more than 30 countries and a small group of corporations with which the Lab has strong ties. A few of them–H-P, Motorola, Intel, and CSK–joined as corporate partners in the effort.

Of course, Pentland and Resnick knew they could not simply replicate in the developing world a method that had worked for companies in the U.S. Knowing that developing countries needed to establish a public policy framework that allowed them to "leapfrog" into the ranks of digitalized counties, MIT reached out to Harvard University's Center for International Development (CID), led by noted economist Jeff Sachs, to gain public policy guidance. This cross-Cambridge academic alliance linked two institutions that had quite different–and some would say opposing–academic cultures when it came to the Internet. While MIT helped solve the technological riddles that led to the Internet and, especially, the World Wide Web, Harvard has been a prominent techno-skeptic. By 1999, at least a dozen programs dotted Harvard's organization chart, each of them critically examining the social implications of the new digital technology. The yin/yang alliance of Harvard/MIT produced a balance of elements, which may explain why it has attracted considerable attention from leaders in the worldwide movement to close the digital divide.[125]

Today, both the MIT and the Harvard researchers are converging in India. A country with a third of the world's poor and one-fourth of the world's software workers, India has become a gathering point and lightening rod for all sorts of experiments in closing the digital divide. Dozens of international organizations and technology-savvy global NGO networks are testing their theories in India regarding the extension of IT to the poor.[126]

---

[125] Both MIT Media Lab and Harvard's CID have been integrated into efforts within the World Bank, the United Nations, and the World Economic Forum to fashion solutions to the digital divide.
[126] See www.digitaldivideindia.org. See also the India Initiative of Digital Partners. (www.DigitalPartners.org).

After collaborating on a project to test affordable ways of using Internet kiosks to empower the poor, MIT and CID's Information Technologies Group collaborated on a much bigger assignment–bringing the Media Lab concept to India. Soon Media Lab Asia was born, with a fresh commitment by the Indian Government for $200 million, which the Lab expects to match many times over through private investments in support of social initiatives that will emerge from its experiments.

Meanwhile, back in Cambridge, MIT Media Lab itself seems to be undergoing a kind of metamorphosis. Teams of Media Lab graduate students, themselves quite multicultural, have moved out in front of their professors to collaborate on a method to design "appropriate technologies" for the poor. Their method, which applies the latest thinking in IT design taught by the Lab, involves launching experiments in non-governmental organizations overseen by academic partnerships, using a methodology called "think cycle."[127] One recent example is of innovative ways to deliver health care to remote villages. Another project involves reducing the costs of data processing by microcredit programs through the use of smart cards.

The Think Cycle project involved extensive outreach to non-governmental organizations in the field working with the poorest of the poor. "In our surveys of NGOs, we weren't interested in finding out what they were doing with the Internet," says Nitin Sawney, a Ph.D. student at the Media Lab and the leader of a group of graduate students who are spearheading the project. "We wanted to know what sort of problems they were facing in delivering clean water to villages or reducing infant mortality, or what to do about typhoid and cholera. We found that a lot of people in the field were tying to establish 'human generated power systems' for locations without electricity."[128]

To translate the problems faced by NGOs addressing rural poverty into technological solutions, Sawney and his colleagues have turned to Open Source technology. "If an innovation is proprietary, it wouldn't be able to elicit the collaboration needed for people to contribute to the design solutions and get the

---

[127] See www.thinkcycle.org.
[128] Interview in Cambridge, MA, 2001.

kinks worked out. "If we are working on a water filter, we have to make sure that those testing the product in the field are free to tell us what works and what doesn't," said Sawney.

Certainly, a wide distance separates academic projects such as Think Cycle from the methods and motives of corporate laboratories. But many at the Media Lab insist that the gap can be closed as companies explore business models that use Open Source approaches and still provide adequate returns on investment.[129] "We're not too concerned with the financial viability of any of this effort yet," he says. "We are trying to give NGOs a virtual R&D arm without worrying if their efforts will attract corporate support. Once we see how basic needs can be filled using the latest technology, it may well be possible to find financial formulas that make it feasible."

It is too early to tell whether corporate research departments that have relied on MIT Media Lab for guidance in the past will eventually incorporate social issues into their own research agendas. But given MIT Media Lab's role in predicting the future of digital technology, few would place bets that it is following the wrong path.

---

[129] Many in the movement to close the digital divide are watching closely a project called Simputer, a computer affordable to low-income persons, accessible in many languages and being developed in Bangalore, India. The project combines the Open Source approach with a business model that offers returns on investment. See www.simputer.org.

CHAPTER EIGHT

Leadership: Responding to Techno-Pessimists

The bulk of the interviews that led to this analysis were conducted with senior managers and middle managers whose perspectives seemed strictly *managerial* and certainly devoid of ideological overtones. Each of them was preoccupied, as corporate managers often are, with how to achieve big impacts with few staff members, financial constraints, and volatile markets. Our conversations with these interview subjects didn't evolve into commentary on broad discussions about the state of world affairs. No one mentioned the anti-globalization protestors who had shut down Seattle's World Trade Organization's Ministerial in 1999 and who appeared again in greater numbers in the Genoa G-8 Summit in 2001. There were no discussions of concerns about inequities within and between countries that were being exacerbated, not diminished, by the rise of digital technology.[130]

Yet, the expressions of digital corporate citizenship depicted in this report, are not just about management. They are also about leadership or, perhaps, a form of "managerial leadership" in which corporate managers feel compelled to formulate a response to big societal issues on behalf of their chief executives. After all, CEOs in the IT sector, whether they liked it or not, had indeed become high-profile world leaders. Get-togethers that involved corporate chiefs and their counterparts in government had become one of the most talked-about issues. A good barometer of this trend is the World Economic Forum

---

[130] For a good analysis of these inequities, and their relationship to digital technology, see *Making Technologies Work for Human Development: The Human Development Report, 2001*, United Nations Development Programme, 2001.

at Davos, Switzerland. By 2002, at WEF's annual gathering held in New York City, a third of the agenda topics addressed some aspect of the digital divide.[131] The topic often came up when CEOs visited prime ministers in China, Brazil, India and other emerging market countries where digital technology had become a focal point for hopes and fears. "Everywhere we go, we are asked to speak on the topic," said Eric Benhamou, chairman of 3Com and Palm. "It has become impossible for any executive in the IT industry not to have a point of view about the digital divide."[132]

The need for a corporate response to the digital divide issue emerged gradually during the course of the 1990s as the dot-com bubble emerged and then burst. Before the digital divide became known in corporate-citizenship circles, it was an issue known only to policy wonks and liberal activists inside the Washington, DC, Beltway. Many of these insiders were given a sympathetic hearing by Vice President Al Gore. Eventually, President Clinton himself made closing the digital divide one of his signature issues.

When the U.S. Department of Commerce held its first conferences on the digital divide in 1994, there were no corporations on the scene. It is not hard to understand why. In the U.S., the mid-1990s clash over the digital divide had all the hallmarks of ideological struggles of the past in which the corporate sector would always assume a defensive posture. As in decades past, liberal activists and their allies in Congress clashed with a few telecommunications corporations and Republican politicians over the social impact of the "new information superhighway," as the Internet was called in the mid-1990s. Activists wanted government regulators to intervene to make sure that the highway would provide "universal access" to the poor. AT&T, MCI, Sprint, and the "Baby Bell" companies pooh-poohed their concerns, arguing that such talk was merely a smokescreen for efforts to hold back the magic of innovation. Upstart computing companies like Microsoft, Sun Microsystems, and Cisco Systems avoided these discussions altogether out of

---

[131] See www.wef.org.
[132] Interview in Santa Clara, Calif., 2001.

concern that they would be engaged in discussions that would lead to onerous new regulations.

Behind this debate were predictions of the impact of the new market forces, which were being unleashed by the Internet.[133] As debates heated up leading to the Telecom Act of 1996, regulators and politicians were forced to ask themselves difficult questions for which they found no easy answers: Are current market incentives sufficient to coax private investors into supporting the needed investments in technology? Will such incentives emerge *later* as computers become cheaper and ubiquitous? Could incentives be *created* through regulation, tax credits, or public subsidy of commercial enterprises? Without good data to resolve such questions, economic philosophy filled the void. Without good research to guide them, regulators and politicians invoked names like Adam Smith and Schumpeter as they pondered whether the new market forces would have a disrupting effect, breaking apart the collusion of today's monopolists without the need for government intervention. It is no surprise, then, that the digital divide debates produced two groupings on either end of the left/right spectrum: the market-pessimists and the market-optimists.

Warnings of the Digital Divide

In the early 1990s, techno-pessimists were in the majority. It is not hard to understand why. At the time, the economy confirmed fears about the impact of the digital revolution on jobs. Disavowing traditions of secure employment, companies shed millions from their workforces. The *New York Times* dramatized the plight of "displaced workers" in a prize-winning series.[134] As billionaires proliferated, a popular book announced the arrival of a "winner-take-all society"[135] destined to help a few while leaving everyone else behind. Secretary of Labor Robert Reich, in *The Work of Nations*, warned that all but high-

---

[133] An excellent assessment of the research documenting the digital divide, which was used by activists to press the case for FCC regulation, is "The Growing Digital Divide: Implications for an Open Research Agenda," by Donna Hoffman and Thomas Novak, Vanderbilt University, November, 29, 1999. See http://ecommerce.vanderbilt.edu/.

[134] See *New York Times*, June 27, 1996.

[135] *The Winner Take All Society*, by Robert Frank and Philip Cook, Free Press, 1995.

end "knowledge workers" would be excluded from benefits of the information age.[136] Freelance author Joel Rifken, in *The End of Work*,[137] warned of massive social dislocations as computerization wipes out armies of service workers, and as advances in biotech decimate employment on small farms. "While some new jobs are being created, they are, for the most part, low paying and generally temporary employment," Rifken conceded.[138]

Adding data to the concern, Rand Corporation, Rutgers University, and several other research institutions conducted surveys on the "digital divide," which referred originally to the gap in connectivity between the information haves and have-nots. (A bookshelf full of studies showed that poor rural dwellers, and especially poor ethnic minorities, have far less access than the middle class or the wealthy to personal computers at home, to the Internet, and to wired classrooms. One study in 1998 pointed out that, although 40 percent of all homes have personal computers, affluent households are seven times more likely to own one than those with household incomes of $10,000 or less. And, even in that poorest category, whites were twice as likely as blacks to own a personal computer.)[139]

Predictions that these disparities will continue to grow in future years were based on two notions: First, that companies and governments will find it unfeasible to pay for upgrading infrastructures in low-end areas, and will thereby exclude the poor from broadband networks. Second, even if the poor are eventually offered access to high-speed telecommunications net-works in their homes, they will be excluded by high user fees. (One study noted that, even after telephone costs declined over the years, over 30 percent of households with income under $10,000 still cannot afford a telephone.[140]) One of the leading investigators of this genre, Rutgers University's Philip Aspden, produced volumes of evidence that point to the "triple barriers

---

[136] *The Work of Nations*, by Robert Reich, Vintage Books, 1992.
[137] *The End of Work*, by Jermy Rifkin, Tarcher/Putnam, 1995.
[138] Interview in Los Angeles, 2000.
[139] See "Falling Through the Net," available from the Benton Foundation at www.digitaldividenetwork.org.
[140] See Hoffman and Novak, http://ecommerce.vanderbilt.edu/.

of price, complexity, and awareness"–all of which keep the poor from turning the Internet into a tool for learning.[141]

Even CEOs made public utterances that seemed to reinforce the pessimists' views. Richard McGinn, CEO of Lucent Technologies, warned of "a two-tiered society...a great divide created by technology."[142] Perhaps the most damning criticism of optimists comes from one of the founders of the MIT Computer Laboratory, the late Michael Dertouzos. In his predictive book, *What Will Be*,[143] he cited figures showing that rich countries spend a higher proportion of their income on information products than poor ones by a factor of ten. He extrapolated that the biggest barrier to the success of the have-nots is that they live in "a culture that fails to value information."[144] He argues that the barrier they face is rooted in the culture of poverty. "They therefore fail to see the worth of spending the time to master information technology, even when access is offered to them." Thus, he concludes, "Left to its own devices, the Information Marketplace will increase the gap between rich and poor countries and between rich and poor people."

The mass media, up through the mid-1990s, agreed with the pessimists. The term "digital divide" found its way into special reports by CNN and the *New York Times*. A 1995 *Newsweek* headline blared, "Computers Deepen Gap between Rich and Poor." Shortly after, on ABC's "Nightline" television program, Ted Koppel examined what he called the "Economic Fallout of the Digital Age," showing how economic prosperity was skewed to upper income groups.[145]

The effect of the outpouring of studies was to support the contention of activists that regulation was needed to redress inequities. The research on the digital divide made three points, which were eventually adopted in the 1996 Telecommunications Act:

---

[141] "Access: Who Is on the Web and Why?" lecture given on Feb. 2, 1998, University of Michigan, Ann Arbor. Available at www.communitytechnology.org/aspden.
[142] Speech at World Economic Forum, 1998.
[143] Michael Dertouzos, *What Will Be: How the New World of Information Will Change Our Lives*, Harper Collins, New York, 1997.
[144] Interview in New York City, 1998.
[145] November 7, 1996.

- First, the concept of "universal service," originally drafted to protect isolated rural citizens, should be continually redefined to combat the growing economic inequities in the digital age.
- Second, even if they are not given immediate access to new broadband communications infrastructures to their homes, the poor needed immediate access to "alternative points of connectivity," such as school or libraries that could serve as a basis for adult education, computer literacy, entrepreneurship, and job training.
- Third, that the question of whether current market incentives could be counted upon to close the digital divide, or whether new market-shaping regulation might be needed, remained an open question. Instead, the federal government put the private sector on notice that it would scrutinize the effects of the market to see if meaningful access were provided to the have-nots as the digital era unfolds.[146]

Thus, in the years following the Telecommunication Act of 1996, the problem of Internet-based inequities simmers as a "backburner" issue that refuses to go away, even though front-burner Internet policies, for example, intellectual property rights, piracy, encryption, or children's rights, grab headlines. "The digital divide is always percolating," says Bill Meyers of the United States Internet Council. "It cross-cuts and under-lies many of the Internet issues being debated in Washington. Everyone knows it just won't go away and that it could burst open into new forms of regulation at any moment."[147]

As it became clear that the federal government was unlikely to redress the digital divide anytime soon, activists took their case to the public at large. One researcher who was influential in broadening concerns regarding the digital divide to the

---

[146] This third point, merely implied in the 1996 Act, was more fully spelled out in a White House directive that "charges the Federal Communications Commission and the states with continuing responsibility to review the definition of universal service" to meet changing social circumstances. The directive also "obliges those who provide telecommunications services to contribute to the preservation and enhancement of universal service." "Administration's Policy Reform Initiative," as quoted by Don Taspscott in *The Digital Economy*, McGraw-Hill, 1997.

[147] Interview in Washington, DC, 1999.

international level was a University of California. Berkeley sociologist, Manuel Castells. His three-volume articulation of the *problematique* of the digital divide remains the most damning criticism of the impact of the new economy on the world's poor.[148]

As activists moved to the international arena, some concentrated on state and local efforts to reign in high-tech giants. A growing network of community-based organizations formed to press for community control of computing, including the Association for Community Technology and Computer Professionals for Social Responsibility.

Searching for a model of regulatory means to restrain the high-tech corporate giants, some activists turned to the state utility commissions. Many of them drew analogies from the Community Reinvestment Act (CRA), passed in 1977, which required merging banks and insurers to show their responsiveness to community needs. That act had been created to counter a practice called "redlining," in which bankers and insurers purportedly "drew a red line" around low-income areas, and then prohibited their managers from lending or investing in such areas. The commitments made by banks and insurance companies to make loans, equity investments, and philanthropic contributions to low-income communities reached over one trillion dollars by 1999– an unprecedented triumph for grassroots activism, which may have dramatically boosted African-American and Hispanic home ownership and led to a big increase in minority-owned businesses. Hoping to have a similar effect on harnessing the high-tech corporations, many activists saw a parallel to what they called "electronic redlining," in which high-tech companies pursued policies that excluded the poor.

During 1997, twin victories at the state level gave activists some ground for hope. The first successful effort by activists to push for CRA-like legislation to close the digital divide came in California amid the merger between SBC Communications and Pacific Bell. The California Public Utilities Commission (CPUC)

---

[148] *The Rise of the Network Society*, Volumes I, II, III, by Manuel Castells, Blackwell Publishers, published between 1996 and 1998. The volumes, written in the style of European grand social theory depicting the interconnected *problematique* of the digital divide, provides a framework for the emergence of the anti-globalization movement and its link to the new information technology.

brokered an arrangement in which Pacific Bell agreed to create a $50 million fund. The money was used to "research ways in which SBC can build commercial markets that meet the practical needs of low-income persons."[149] A few months later, activists won a similar victory in Illinois. After SBC Corporation sought a green light for its acquisition of Ameritech, community leaders won support for a plan for a $200 million fund just like the one in California.

But no other CRA-like initiatives were presented to state utility commissions. With the onset of the Bush era, most insiders in the field of community economic development admit that circumstances in the early 21st century are not analogous those of 1977. "Today's high-tech industries are already highly consolidated, unlike banks and insurance companies which, in 1977, had not yet been engulfed in two decades of mergers and acquisitions. There simply are no models of activism that seem feasible now," lamented Bart Harvey, President of the Enterprise Foundation, a national nonprofit that played a major role in the passage of CRA legislation a generation earlier.[150] In recent years, as the federal government embraced the philosophy of deregulation, continuation of the CRA itself has been cast into doubt. New CRA-like initiatives have not been entertained at the federal level.

The Ascendance of Optimists

After the passage of the U.S. Telecommunications Act of 1996, the market optimists clearly held sway. In fact, the Act confirmed a view that had long been argued by conservatives–that the market, not government controls, must be the basis for any further solution for the information have-nots. While the Act stressed the value of extending the information superhighway to the poor, the Federal Communications Commission in the Clinton era asserted that government would not be the major funder of that effort. In fact, the Act sought to undo the cross-subsidy arrangements that, in the past, forced telephone companies to support low-income consumers with profits obtained from the affluent.

---

[149] Interview with Donald Vial, former chair of CPUC, in San Francisco, 1999.
[150] Interview in Washington, DC, 1998.

Even the provision that most pleased the pessimists–the creation of a $2 billion annual "E-Rate" fund to subsidize purchase of telecommunications equipment for schools, libraries, and rural health care centers–relied on markets to serve low-income consumers.[151] Though widely embraced by the educational community, the E-rate plan ran into political snags. Conservative members of Congress called it a hidden tax whose costs would be ultimately borne by consumers.[152]

Indeed, the Act reframed universal service for the first time in the context of the sweeping effort to promote innovation and competition in telecommunications. By so doing, it encouraged reformers to reframe their antipoverty programs in terms consistent with the dynamic forces of the market. It pointed to a future in which activists and regulators, as much as the employees of high-tech companies, are all involved in "market-building."

As Internet stocks led the Dow to all-time highs in the late 1990s, it became more difficult to gain a hearing for arguments that dispute the wisdom of the market. Just as economic conditions in the early 1990s gave fuel to the digital skeptics, the late 1990s gave credence to digital utopians.

In 1996, Bill Gates became the first corporate chief executive to contradict the logic of the pessimists. His book, *The Road Ahead*, is a manifesto to the optimists' position. In it he states flatly, "The gap between the haves and have-nots will diminish."[153] (The only evidence he offered to back up his assertion was that, in the future, jobs in information technology could be easily transferred to low-cost workers in poor countries.)

But in subsequent years others have filled in the missing logic. In 1997, an influential consultant named Peter Schwartz wrote an essay in *Wired*, "The Long Boom,"[154] which went beyond previous predictions that the digital economy would

---

[151] An ingenious aspect of this provision is that it included incentives for institutions serving low-income constituencies: the poorer their clients, the deeper their discounts–up to a 90 percent mark-down for institutions serving the poorest of the poor.
[152] In mid-1998, the FCC scaled back the E-rate plan by about 40 percent.
[153] *The Road Ahead*, Bill Gates, Penguin Books, 1997, p. 297.
[154] "The Long Boom," was later developed into a book, *The Long Boom: A Vision for the Coming Age of Prosperity*, by Peter Schwartz, Peter Leyden, and Joel Hyatt, Perseus Press, 2000. It argues that "the world has steadily been getting better."

bring sustained low unemployment and low inflation. He said, "We are riding the early waves of a 25-year run of a greatly expanding economy...that will do much to solve seemingly intractable problems like poverty." Bucking conventional wisdom, he predicted that the inequities will be overcome as public and private sectors both realize that "it pays to get everyone tied to the information grid."[155]

Schwartz' thesis had legs. A full year later, the *New York Times* ran a full-page article analyzing Schwartz's views. In August 1998, in its cover story, *Business Week*[156] ignored troubles in Japan and Russia to predict a "Rising Tide" economy that would lift all boats. The article quoted statistics from the Economic Policy Institute that show that the long-term decline in median worker wages has been reversed.

The reason for the positive assessment was new economic statistics: The highest income gains came from the poorest workers, bringing a sharp decline in the numbers who are on welfare. In May 1999, the Department of Labor revealed that unemployment had reached a thirty-year low of 4.2 percent and that the biggest employment gains were among blacks, at a historic low of 7.7 percent, while Hispanics were at near-historic lows of 6.9 percent.

Said *Business Week*, "With the economy continuing to expand, companies are snapping up minorities, women, seniors, and anyone else willing to work for a day's pay...Technology has become a powerful force for greater equality." The media did much to dispel the public's fears. "The seven regional telephone companies had slashed some 125,000 jobs, on top of the 40,000 latest cuts announced at AT&T. Nevertheless, the industry's total employment rose by 91,000 during the period, as companies beefed up employment in cellular and other fast-growing businesses," claimed *Business Week*.[157]

Other studies suggested that, more than anticipated, low-income persons were going to community colleges, vocational

---

[155] Ibid., p. 2.
[156] "The Economy's Rising Tide," by David Leonhardt, *Business Week*, April 26, 1999. The article explained that in the new economy businesses are being forced to train their "rawest recruits," turning them into knowledge workers.
[157] *Business Week*, March 11, 1996.

schools, or reaping the benefits of on-the-job training to get the computer skills they needed to be employable. For example, a 1998 report by a group of Harvard economists, Lawrence Katz, Claudia Golin, and David Uster and Alan Kreuger of Princeton attributed 30 to 50 percent of the increase in demand for workers in the past 25 years to the computer. What is more, their research showed that most of these jobs were not occupied by those with specialized skills. In fact, many companies benefited by creating new jobs that use simplified software, require fewer technical skills, and are therefore accessible to low-skilled workers.

A Pragmatic Middle Way?

With the sudden decline of technology stocks in 2001, and the rise of the Bush Presidency, the upbeat mood has been replaced by a more nuanced perspective. "The new view is that the market is likely to increase *some* aspects of the digital divide and *reduce* others," says Charles Firestone, director of the Aspen Institute's Communications and Society program.[158] Some recent studies show that women and ethnic minorities, for example, seem to be signing on to the Internet at a faster rate than white males.[159] On the other hand, recent data from the United Nations Development Programme have shown that, in the past decade as technology increasingly drives world trade, the share of total world trade conducted by the poorest 50 percent was cut in half.[160]

Even private sector leaders are willing to concede that the public sector may have to join forces with leaders of academia and non-governmental organizations to harness market forces for the have-nots. Steve Case, then-CEO of America Online (now AOL Time Warner) in 1997 became the first top IT executive to challenge his peers attending that year's World Economic Forum to join together in a period of intense exploration and experimentation in the use of digital technology by public policymakers. "We should work with governments to unleash innovations that close the digital divide as intensively as we

---

[158] Interview in Washington, DC, 1999.
[159] See the U.S. Department of Commerce site containing data on the digital divide, www.ntia.doc.gov/ntiahome/digitaldivide.
[160] Human Development Report, United Nations Development Programme, 2000.

worked together to promote commercial innovation in the previous decade," he said.[161]

In the last years of the Clinton era, the federal mood seemed to anticipate the arrival of George W. Bush by calling for a period of study on the social impact of technology, rather than launch into further federally funded social experiments. The contemplative mood was best expressed in a report published in February 1999 by the President's Commission on Information Technology, composed equally of corporate executives and academic computer scientists. After calling attention to the positive social transformations that could be achieved by society's transition into the digital age, the report argued on behalf of proposals to earmark $100 million over five years in an effort to understand "social impacts" of technology.[162]

As if to undermine complacency in the private sector, the Clinton White House's main advisor on digital divide matters underscored the point following the passage of the act: "We're waiting to see if the private sector takes the leadership to voluntarily assure that the benefits of technology are broadly shared. If they do so, they will be able to avoid further regulation."[163]

When President Bush came into office, the hands-off mood of the federal government was merely reinforced. In his first press conference after becoming the Bush's new chairman of the Federal Communications Commission, Michael Powell (son of Secretary of State Colin Powell), summarily rejected the possibility that the FCC would seek new regulation to contain high-tech businesses. Still, the topic of the digital divide had become a global issue, not a national one. Clearly, the ball was now in the court of the corporations. Are they willing to shift their own corporate cultures to be responsive to the poor on a voluntary basis? It was time for leaders to step forth from the corporate sector to show the way.

---

[161] Speech at World Economic Forum, Davos, Switzerland, 1997.

[162] Report to the President, February 24, 1999, President's Committee on Information Technology. For a copy of the report, see www.ccic.gov/ac/report.

[163] Interview with Thomas Kahil, White House advisor, in Washington, DC, 1998.

CHAPTER NINE

Conclusion: What We Know and What We Don't

This report's analysis of the corporate-citizenship efforts of leading high-tech corporations allows us to draw just a few conclusions. More significantly, it allows us to ponder what we *don't* know. Knowing what we don't know may be more important. It allows the reader to frame some important questions about the future of corporate citizenship–about the ability of corporations to respond effectively to the looming issue of the digital divide.

What We *Do* Know

Whereas the practice of "strategic corporate citizenship" predates the rise of the converged Internet corporations, these companies seem to have taken the practice further by leveraging their technology and their management systems to create sizable, high-impact projects at minimal out-of-pocket cost to themselves. For example, they have been able to leverage their certification programs conducted in partnership with community colleges to formulate job-training programs that serve economic-development goals. They have been able to justify as an internal marketing expense visionary efforts to match millions of volunteers to causes seeking volunteers. Other on-line marketers, seeking the key to customer loyalty, have been effective in reaching out to nonprofit organizations to build a sense of community into their web sites. Washington, DC, offices of high-tech corporations employ nonprofit organizations to build a mood in Washington to accelerate government's investment in broadband or other policies conducive to high-tech interests. "We have achieved a seamless integration between philanthropy and corporate strategy," said Samme Thompson, Senior Vice President of Motorola.[164] Since the days of Henry Ford, that alignment between doing good and doing well has been a long-sought goal–but one that may have only recently been achievable with the help of digital technology.

The companies' signature initiatives represent the visible tip of the iceberg in the companies' relationships with nonprofit organizations. Beneath the surface, many of the companies' business units and functions have for pragmatic reasons created their own ties with nonprofit organizations. The extent of these relationships causes the author to propose the hypothesis that new-economy corporations have more extensive–and more broadly distributed–relationships with nonprofit organizations than old-economy companies, whereby traditional nonprofits are more likely to be relegated to the companies' philanthropic foundations. Indeed, the interviews conducted for this report suggest that even young high-tech companies have established an *infrastructure* of nonprofit relationships spread throughout their corporate culture.

Whether companies have been able to translate this nonprofit infrastructure into visionary social initiatives depends to a great degree on the role of senior to mid-level managers– typically those at the senior vice president level or below–who are clearly playing a starring role as authors of signature initiatives. It is their job to balance the interests of several internal departments and to join ideas, budgets, and management skills in the formulation of internal partnerships that are bigger than the sum of the parts. Since the era of downsizing in the late 1980s recession, mid-managers have taken a bad rap; hundreds of thousands of them have been eliminated from organization charts amid the constant corporate reinventions of the 1990s. But many of them interviewed for this report clearly see their calling as bridge builders. "Our job is to balance the headquarters perspective with the operational people in the field. We're close enough to the CEO to frame a project in large terms, but we're close enough to operations to

---

[164] Interview in Chicago, IL, 2001.

know what can be implemented and what can't," said one interviewee on condition of anonymity.

What We *Don't* Know

We don't know the future of these efforts, or even the entire spectrum of corporate citizenship efforts. Most of these interviews were conducted in the heady atmosphere of the late 1990s, where companies were enjoying constantly escalating stock prices, and an ideology prevailed that suggested that the dot-coms owned the future. That era quickly disappeared between 2000 and 2002, when Silicon Valley experienced its worse slump in its 50-year history. In 2001, venture capital dropped 71 percent from the preceding year, and most of that has been spent merely keeping struggling companies alive. Just as many experimental projects once entertained by venture capitalists have been scrapped, it is hard to imagine that corporate citizenship could flourish in such an atmosphere.

Or could it? "I know it is counter-intuitive," said Steven Zeilke, a Motorola manager who has spent several years building internal support for a corporate initiative that adapts Motorola's products and services so that they meet the needs of rural villagers around the world. "But social initiatives are the key to our company's future success."

Without offering a prediction, the author concludes with a presentation of five scenarios. They suggest alternative futures, both pessimistic and hopeful, for high-tech corporate citizenship and for the companies themselves.

The "Social Adventurism" Model. This is the possibility that today's visionary initiatives may become tomorrow's unaffordable luxury. No matter how much they are defended by CEOs today as making good business sense, they may be dismissed as mere "social adventurism" in the future by decision makers intent to demonstrating their lean-mean tactics. In this scenario, the internal advocates who pushed for these initiatives will be marginalized or forced into retirement, and their visionary ideas will become erased from the corporate memory.

The Return-to-Philanthropy Model. Social initiatives that were initially conceived as serving goals will be "philanthropized" into corporate foundations or even spun off as initiatives supported by the personal philanthropy of chairmen, CEOs, and other wealthy executives. In some cases, projects that had hoped to emerge as business units might attract support from multilateral aid agencies or other forms of subsidy. In a number of cases, prominent CEOs–Microsoft's Bill Gates, AOL Time Warner's Steve Case, Dell Computer's Michael Dell, Oracle's Larry Ellison, and Gateway's Ted Waitt–have each made personal gifts that matched or exceeded the funding spent on social initiatives conceived by their own corporations. Just as the Bill & Melinda Gates Foundation transformed Microsoft's Library project into a much larger library-and-education initiative conducted by the Gates' private foundation, other CEOs may also use their own companies as test laboratories for their personal philanthropy.

Cross-Functionalism Model. In this case, mid-managers will rescue social initiatives by becoming even more adept at forging creative internal alliances that support many internal goals at once. This report shows that nonprofit organizations can emerge as the least expensive or most effective partners to achieve business goals. By establishing new ways of measuring the benefits of signature initiatives, their advocates may be able to defend them effectively to skeptical chief financial officers and CEOs.

The Innovation Model. This is the scenario in which companies will increasingly call upon their corporate social initiatives as a way of bringing innovation to the corporation, the approach labeled by Rosabeth Moss Kanter as "beta testing in the social sector." Given the important need to formulate new business models to serve billions of consumers in the developing world, one could easily imagine that this approach to innovation will become increasingly recognized.

The Profit Center Model. In this scenario, the company's social initiatives will eventually be established as profitable internal business or even sold off as separate companies with their own chance for becoming publicly traded corporations. We have seen that some high-tech companies have explicitly defined the aims of their social initiatives so that they pay for themselves. An example is Real Networks, whose RealActive subsidiary charges fees to activists groups to become more adept at using web sites to their advantage. The greatest opportunities for the success of such "double bottom line"[165] initiatives may be in the developing world. This is the approach of Telenor, the Norwegian telecommunications corporation, which is 51 percent owner of a Bangladeshi wireless business called Grameen Phone (GP). GP is widely lauded by NGOs and public policy officials for its innovative approach to fostering entrepreneurship and economic-development in impoverished rural villages.

In one of the GP programs, conducted by Bangladesh's highly touted Grameen Bank, village "phone ladies" are given credit to buy wireless phones, which they in turn rent to villagers who use the phones to become more productive in running their own microbusinesses. Grameen Phone, which also serves more affluent customers in Bangladesh, expects to generate a $25 million profit in 2001, after only five years in operation. The initiative has already attracted $130 million in investment from public and private sources. "It shows that even the most visionary IT business could be established as a sound business proposition," says Iqbal Quadir, the founder of Grameen Phone.[166]

Whichever future comes to pass, the stakes are large. If the companies succeed in their efforts to reach out to nonprofits and, beyond, to the disenfranchised masses, their own fortunes may well be sustainable. If not, it is easy to imagine that the obstacles in front of them will continue to mount.

---

[165] The term refers to projects that offer returns on investment using both financial and social criteria.
[166] Interview in Cambridge, MA, 2001.

Annotated Bibliography

This review of literature, amplifying and expanding on references and footnotes integrated into the text, contains a selection of materials divided into the following sections:

1. Social Theory of the Digital Revolution
2. Cross-Sector Partnerships
3. E-Development
4. High-Tech Corporate Management
5. High-Tech Corporate Community Relations
6. High-Tech Marketing and the Public Interest
7. High-Tech R&D and the Public Interest
8. High-Tech Human Resources Management and the Public Interest
9. High-Tech Corporate Government Affairs and the Public Interest

1. Social Theory of the Digital Revolution

Throughout the 1990s and into the new millennium, a number of writers from within and without academia have offered explanations of the peculiar dynamics of the digital paradigm and its implications for business. Some of them have gone further by assessing the broader societal dynamics of the digital economy and its challenges to the "social sphere," including government, education and social causes. Since the dot-com bust in mid-2000, most of the authors in this genre explain the excesses of the earlier period of dot-com mania. Many of these have emphasized the recessionary period of 2000-2002 as a time of reflection and policy formation. Some of them call for new approaches to governance in which the digital revolution is harnessed to lessen the inequities that had been exacerbated in the earlier period.

A Brief History of the Future: From Radio Days to Internet Years in a Lifetime, by John Naughton, New York, Overlook, 1999.
> Naughton explains the evolution of technologies that led to the creation of the Internet and, in the process, suggests how the "open society" values common to the nonprofit sector have been integrated into the technological solutions that created the World Wide Web.

The Control Revolution: How the Internet is Putting Individuals in Charge and Changing the World We Know, by Andrew Shapiro, New York, Century Foundation, 1999.
> Shapiro argues that the fundamental aspect of the changes being wrought by the information revolution is that individuals are able to free themselves from institutional controls and gain a broader degree of control over their lives than was possible in the old economy.

Connexity: How To Live in a Connected World, by Geoff Mulgan, Boston, Harvard Business School Press, 1997.
> Mulgan addresses how the dynamics of the digital economy intensifies the interdependence between individuals and between institutions in society.

Democracy and Technology, edited by Richard Sclove, New York, Gilford Press, 1995.
> The articles contribute to a framework for how communities can harness the power of technology to shape their destinies.

Digital Divide: Computers in Our Children's Future, by David Bolt and Ray Crawford, New York, TV Books, 2000.
> With a U.S. focus, the authors provide superficial treatment of the digital divide issue in the U.S. with an emphasis on ethnic perspectives. However, the book includes a useful summary of statistics on disparities between rich and poor. Some of these are growing, while others are diminishing, as the digital era proceeds.

The Digital Divide: Facing a Crisis or Creating a Myth? edited by Benjamin Compaine, Cambridge, MA, MIT Press.
> The writers look at the U.S. perspectives on the digital divide and suggest that some gaps are diminishing over time.

Digital McLuhan:A Guide to the Information Millennium, by Paul Linson, New York, Routledge, 1999.
> The author sees the digital revolution as fostering the fulfillment of Marshall McLuhan's vision of the "global village," articulated in 1964 in Understanding Media. The author also revisits McLuhan's thesis to create a framework for discussing whether society will be able to shape the digital future or if it will be inevitably shaped by the determinism of technology itself.

The Follies of Globalization Theory, by Justin Rosenberg, London Verso, 2000.
> Rosenberg explains how the academic examination of "globalization" grew from the field of international relations and why the leading thinkers of this field have erred in their efforts to explain how globalization works.

Fostering Research on the Economic and Social Impacts of Information Technology, Washington, National Research Council, 1998.
> Increasingly, the U.S. federal government is integrating investigations into the social impact of computing into its technology research agenda. This series of essays from a 1997 research council workshop defines questions and methodologies that are now being employed by the National Science Foundation to consider social impacts of technology and how they can be mitigated.

Future Positive: International Cooperation in the 21st Century, by Michael Edwards, Earthscan, London, 2000.
> The book explains how the intergovernmental system is changing to accommodate the champions of globalization in the market economy as well as the critics of globalization in civil society movements. Though the book does not address the dynamics of the digital revolution per se, it helps to formulate a framework about how the digital age may reinforce the reinvention of global governance that the author sees reflected in a number of contemporary trends.

High-technology and Low-Income Communities, edited by Donald Schon, et al., Cambridge, MA, MIT Press, 1999.
> This is a disparate collection of essays with little connecting framework.

The Highwaymen: Warriors of the Information Superhighway, by Ken Auletta, New York, Harcourt Brace, 1997.
> The book chronicles the experiences of today's high-tech and media moguls and suggests how their style of deal-making and leadership is reshaping society.

The Information Age: Economy, Society and Culture, three-volume series, by Manuel Castells, Blackwell Publishers, Malden, MA, 1997.
> A sociologist, Castells was the first in his discipline to attempt a comprehensive assessment of the problems as well as the possibilities entailed in society's transition into the digital paradigm. The problem is that the bonds of identity and community are being broken, leading to the breakdown of the old social order. Of the three volumes, the one that deals most directly with the impact of technology is volume one, which provides an astute analysis of the way in which information technology is interdependent with globalization.

Information Rules: A Strategic Guide to the Networked Economy, by Carl Shapiro and Hal Varian, Harvard Business School Press, Boston, 1999.
> The authors attempt to explain the economic rules of the information economy and how they translate into business strategies. Their views were influential in helping to undermine the federal government's commitment to using regulation to assure universal access to the Internet. Instead, the authors emphasized that market principles seem adequate to achieve universal service.

The Invisible Continent: Four Strategic Imperatives of the New Economy, by Keniche Ohmae, New York, HarperBusiness, 2000.
> The author is one of the leading exponents of corporate globalization. His earlier volume, *Borderless World,* suggests the opportunities available to companies that establish global strategies, rather than merely extend their domestic operations

abroad. The "invisible continent" is not merely cyberspace but a new culture of interdependence that is changing politics, social interactions, and commerce. He suggests the challenge of establishing business models that are in turn with the evolving digital culture.

Living at Light Speed: Your Survival Guide to Life on the Information Superhighway, by Danny Goodman, New York, Random House, 1994.

Writing at the dawning of networked communications, Goodman explains theories of the "up side" and the "dark side" of their impact on society.

Meganet: How the Global Communications Network Will Connect Everyone on Earth, by Wilson Dizard, Jr., Boulder, CO, Westview Press, 1997.

In an insightful chapter on the "Tele-Have-Nots," the author discusses strategic and tactical challenges for bringing Internet connectivity to Asia, Latin America, and Africa. He examines the widespread thesis that governments in developing countries are being forced to privatize their inefficient telecommunications monopolies out of pressure to become economically competitive. This point of view is an underpinning for the view that telephone service in poor countries will eventually become cheap enough and of sufficiently high quality to allow Internet ubiquity. He also discusses options for wireless approaches to Internet connectivity in the developing world as well as models for the use of satellites to bring the wireless Internet to remote parts of the world.

New Rules for the New Economy: Radical Strategies for a Connected World, by Kevin Kelly, New York, Viking, 1998.

Kelly emphasizes the role of the new economy in "amplifying relationships," and suggests that the value of technology is in the relationships it can build. The implication for the field of corporate citizenship is that, by building relationships that add value, corporate citizenship can be particularly important to high-tech corporations.

One World, Ready or Not: The Manic Logic of Global Capitalism, by William Grieder, New York, Simon & Schuster, 1997.

> The author argues that the digital economy is reinforcing trends that cause the strategies of nation-states to be ineffectual and that allow multinational corporations to avoid efforts by governments to contain them. He also explains why globalization is leading to an excess supply of goods and services, exerting downward pressure on prices and wages. He argues that multinational corporations are no longer guided by the national interests of their country of origin. He opens the reality that new forms of governance are needed to allow the new economy to be sustainable.

Preparing for the Twenty-First Century, by Paul Kennedy, New York, Random House, 1993.

> After writing *The Rise and Fall of Great Powers*, Kennedy put the recent rise of multinational corporations into historical context and pondered the implications of the inability of nation-states to impose standards of corporate social responsibility on the largest multinationals.

The Road Ahead by Bill Gates, New York, Penguin, 1995.

> In presenting his view of the rosy future of a world transformed by digital technology, Bill Gates claimed that the digital divide would resolve itself, citing the evidence that jobs in the digital economy will move to low-cost providers. His main comments on the role of government in this transition are to emphasize it as primary supporter of public education programs that provide the human resources needed.

School Reform in the Information Age, by Howard Mehlinger, Bloomington, Center for Excellence in Education (Indiana University), 1995.

> Mehlinger defined the ways in which new technologies may fulfill long-frustrated possibilities for school reform in its various dimensions.

Telecosm: How Infinite Bandwidth Will Revolutionize Our World, by George Guilder, New York, Free Press, 2000.

> Gilder, perhaps the most influential intellectual cheerleader for the digital revolution, hails the end of the computer era and the rise of a new business paradigm based on infinitely

expanding bandwidth. He discards social and political trends in his analyses, which may explain why he justified the high stock valuations paid for leading high-tech companies during the dot-com boom years. But his inability to weigh these factors lessened the value of his predictions. In this book for example, he cites Global Crossing, which raised billions of dollars to lay cable across the Atlantic, as "one of the companies operating at a scale and imagination that could change the industry, if not the economy."[167] Yet, less than two years after this book was published, Global Crossing was bankrupt, the most dramatic business failure in the dot-com bust.

Technopoly: The Surrender of Culture to Technology by Neil Postman, New York, Vintage Books, 1993.
Postman's views created a framework that has led to a critical body of research on impact of technology on culture. His point of view was later echoed by Sun Microsystems Chief Researcher Bill Joy, who has warned that technology has a determining impact on culture.

Understanding the Digital Economy: Data, Tools and Research, edited by Erik Brynjolfsson and Brain Kahin, Cambridge, MA, MIT Press, 2000.
The editors look at various fields–employment, education, economic development, etc. –and consider the methodological challenges of tracking and analyzing the digital economy.

When Corporations Rule the World, by David Korten, Hartford, Kumarian Press, 1995.
A corporate critic, Korten integrates and sums up the anti-globalists' critique of the role of multinational corporations without making a distinction between new-economy and old-economy companies. He argues that the convergence of technology and pro-market political forces are producing a quantum leap in the power of a small number of corporations. He sees civil society movements as an alternative force, filling the void in values and civic engagement being created as multinationals exert greater influence.

---

[167] p. 276.

Which World: Scenarios for the 21st Century, by Allen Hammond, Washington DC, Island Press, 1998.

> This book, by the Chief Information Officer of the World Resources Institute, underscores our dramatic turning point in history in which we are faced with a sharp alternative: environmental and economic collapse or harnessing technology for sustainable development. Hammond later became one of the articulators of "Digitally Informed Development," expressed in an article in *Foreign Affairs*, and he is implementing his approach to public/private partnership in a WRI web site, digitaldividend.org.

Winner-Take-All Society, by Robert Frank and Philip Cook, New York, Penguin Books, 1995.

> This book is the first to point out that the digital economy contains dynamics that reward a few winning companies disproportionately. Its findings were later reinforced by marketing studies of Forrester Research, which surmised that as few as 50 leading companies would survive as portals to the Internet, while millions of others would be assigned to tiny niche markets.

2. Cross-Sector Partnerships

Since the end of the Cold War, the view has been commonly expressed that governments can no longer be the drivers of social policy, but that business, academia and nonprofit organizations must all be engaged in efforts to formulate and implement policy. Given the power of multinational corporations, the topic of collaboration between corporations and nonprofit organizations has become the object of increasing inquiry.

The Collaboration Challenge: How Nonprofits and Businesses Succeed Through Strategic Alliances, by James Austin, Jossey-Bass Publishers, 2000.

> Prof. Austin, who directs the Social Enterprise Program within Harvard Business School, focuses on factors that lead to successful partnerships between nonprofit organizations and corporations. Although he doesn't address how the dynamics of IT influence such partners, some of the best-practice

examples in his book are drawn from the digital sector, such as that between AOL and Jumpstart.

Crossover Between Nonprofit and Business Sectors, Sasakawa Peace Foundation, 1994.
> This is a report from a fascinating seminar, in which management expert Peter Drucker was a featured speaker. It is also one of the first formal discussions about "corporate/nonprofit" partnerships. In one of the commentaries, a professor at Hitostubashi University named Ikuyo Kaneko, notes that the value of such partnerships is that they provide a new way for businesses to establish relationships that can yield greater success in establishing strategic advantage.

3. E-Development

Since the end of World War II, a massive global effort has been mounted to promote "development," referring to interventions into the economic and social structures of non-affluent countries aimed at helping them enter the ranks of advanced nations. A global network of multilateral and bilateral institutions is in place to foster and track development initiatives. A wide body of research guides this process. Since the mid-1990s, these efforts have been seeking to come to terms with the digital revolution. Some analysts argue that digital technologies imply a total rethinking of development strategies, a point of view referred to as "e-development."

Development and the Information Age, by John Howkins and Robert Valentin, International Development Research Centre, Ottawa, 1998.
> The report from a United Nations seminar uses scenario planning techniques to foresee the impact of information technology on developing countries. Its assessment is that countries that foster transparency and good governance will be able to leapfrog over advanced countries. Those that fail to do so will be left behind.

Development as Freedom, by Amartya Sen, Anchor Books, Random House, New York, 1999.
> Nobel laureate Sen's influential work seeks to undermine the argument by Singapore's Lee Kuan Yew and others who posit

"Asian values" against the values of freedom. He argues that advances in a country's development cannot be achieved without advancing a country's freedom. Since writing this book, several other authors within the Indian diaspora, such as C.K. Prahalad, have argued that Sen's thesis can be fulfilled by "e-development" in which internet infrastructures can be used to bring openness as well as economic development to even very poor regions of the developed world.

"Extending Access to the Digital Economy to Rural and Developing Regions," by Heather Hudson, in *Understanding the Digital Economy: Data, Tools and Research,* edited by Erik Brynjolfsson and Brain Kahin, Cambridge, MA, MIT Press, 2000
The article analyzes strategies for extending and financing Internet infrastructure access to digital technologies in low-income areas. She also makes the case for the importance of access.

The Global Information Technology Report: 2001-2002, edited by Geoffrey Kirkman et al.,New York, Oxford University Press, 2002.
This comprehensive volume, which comes from the Information Technology Group within Harvard's Center for International Development, examines the IT dynamics in 80 countries and then ranks. It considers the degree to which each has polices and practices in place that make them "ready for the networked world." The data is preceded by articles that put the information in context. Though the book does not make policy prescriptions, it is the most exhaustive study to date presenting a view of the world's transition towards information societies and the obstacles and incentives that now shape efforts in the developing world to harness technology for their own use.

Human Development Report, New York, United Nations Development Programme, 1999, 2000, 2001.
Over three years, the UNDP has integrated statistics and analysis on digital technologies' use in the developing world in these annual volumes, which became widely cited references by those seeking the formulas to close the digital divide. The UNDP analysis suggests that the digital divide in growing in some ways and being reduced in others, but that active intervention is needed to make digital markets work

for the poor. The volumes also mark a change of identity for the UNDP, formerly a bastion of anti-market views, as a market-friendly champion of "e-development," referring to efforts to re-engineer policies for sustainable development in light of the new information technology. The volumes were the first to frame the movement to close the divide as a response to critics of globalization. In the 2001 volume, it opened up the relationship between the uneven spread of technologies and the need for a new approach to global governance.

"The Long Boom: A History of the Future: 1980-2020, by Peter Schwartz, *Wired Magazine*, July 1997.
    The article, written at the peak of the era of dot-com utopianism, predicted a future in which the digital era would eliminate poverty, thanks to the way in which new technology would transform government and education.

4. High-Tech Corporate Management

By the early 1990s, business writers and researchers espoused the point of view that the digital economy was producing a new dynamic of business strategy, which implied new approaches to management and leadership. As computer, telecommunications, and media industries converged through mergers and acquisitions, these authors spoke of a digital paradigm in business that is spreading beyond technology industries towards finance, consumer products, retail, and other industries whose practices were being transformed by the Internet.

The Digital Economy: Promise and Peril in the Age of Networked Intelligence, by Don Tapscott, New York, McGraw-Hill, 1995.
    Tapscott coined many of the terms that have become commonplace in explaining why the digital economy operates according to rules that are different from the old economy. One of these is "disintermediation," which refers to old middle-man functions that are eliminated as companies take advantage of the new technology. Though his views have lost traction since the dot-com bust, the ideas presented in this book are still a starting point for researchers seeking to examine the management challenges of high-tech corporations in the new economy. He emphasizes, in particular, the need

for the transformation of the human resources function of corporations and the new leadership role of CEOs, who must devise new perspectives that help government address the public policy challenges in the digital environment.

"The End of Corporate Imperialism," by C. K. Prahalad and Kenneth Lieberthal, *Harvard Business Review on Corporate Strategy*, Boston, Harvard Business School Press, 1992.

This article was the first and still is the best at arguing that, as multinational corporations re-engineer themselves to be competitive in India, China, and other emerging markets, they must fully remake themselves to be relevant to the very different customer needs within the developing world. The authors argue that programs for cultural sensitivity, or just hiring locals, will not be enough. Companies must fundamentally alter their products and services in a way that will transform their first-world operations as well.

Harvard Business Review on Managing High-Tech Industries, Harvard Business School Press, Boston, 1993.

This is one of the first books to argue that corporate management must be radically altered to account for the dynamics of the digital revolution, for example, by enhancing the role of innovation in management, achieving integration between disparate units, and positioning the company for next-generation products. This framework is well represented in corporate "signature initiatives," such as Hewlett-Packard's e-Inclusion in which companies turn to nonprofit organizations for help in developing their next-generation products.

"Innovation Through the Integration of *Technology, Policy and Management*," by Giampiero E.G. Beroggi, in Technology Policy and Management, London, Vol. 1, No. 1, 2001.

This article defines the framework for a new academic journal. The publication presents research papers that look at the intersection between technology, policy, and management. In the digital age, all three elements are changing so rapidly that efforts to catch the intersection between them are crucial to understanding the benefits to society.

Peer-to-Peer: Harnessing the Power of Disruptive Technologies, edited by Andy Oram, Cambridge, MA, O'Reilly, 2001.
Examining Internet operations such as Napster and other approaches that challenge top-down business models, the authors consider how entrepreneurs can tap open code and peer-to-peer technologies to shape businesses that challenge the giants.

"Strategies for the Bottom of the Pyramid: Creating Sustainable Development," by C.K. Prahalad and S.L. Hart, Draft Paper, August, 1999.
This article argues that multinational corporations–old-economy companies as well as new-economy companies–will find profit breakthroughs by serving low-income consumers among the bottom four billion world population. But to succeed, they must radically reinvent their products and services to fit into the way of life of the poor. He also argues that multinationals are essential for generating the investment, management know-how, and scale needed to bridge the digital divide.

The Virtual Corporation: Structuring and Revitalizing the Corporation for the 21st Century by William Davidow and Michael Malone, New York, HarperBusiness, 1992.
This prescient book points to the crucial role of middle management in restructured high-tech corporations. Once a corporation becomes deconstructed into a family of discrete business units and functions, it faces the challenge of fostering cross-functional alliances. It is the role of middle managers to form and manage these internal coalitions, which in some cases produce high-profile social initiatives.

5. High-Tech Corporate Community Relations

Since the late 1980s, the dominant theme in the literature on corporate philanthropy has been its role within corporate strategy. Originally, this theme was referred to as enlightened self-interest, which referred to a vague relationship between doing good and doing well. Recently, considerations of the role of corporate giving (or corporate community relations) have become more focused. In the late 1990s, considerable literature has emerged offering measurement tools, methodologies for building the "business case" for corporate citizenship, and detailed assessments of internal relationships between giving departments and other internal departments that address related management functions. For example, studies now exist on the "bilateral" relationship between philanthropy and marketing, philanthropy and employee management, philanthropy and brand management, and other specific effects. Although most of this literature has not isolated the digital dynamics in corporate community relations, a few studies have pointed out trends in community relations influenced by digital technology.

"Astride the Digital Divide," by Stephen Greene, *Chronicle of Philanthropy*, January 11, 2001.

> The article provides examples of high-tech product donations by digital corporations within a discussion of how nonprofits are building their capacity to handle digital technology.

Benchmarking for International Corporate Community Involvement, Boston, Center for Corporate Community Relations at Boston College/Probus Limited, 2001.

> This report used a total quality management methodology to examine the companies that have achieved "best practices" in mastering various management challenges peculiar to corporate citizenship.

Beyond Access: A Foundation Guide to Ending the Organizational Divide, By Bethay Robertson, published by National Committee for Responsive Philanthropy, Washington DC, 2001.

> The study examines 767 technology grants made by corporate and private foundations and examines trends. The assessment underscores the frustration of nonprofits that they are given ample access to technology but lack the training to use it effectively to build organizational effectiveness.

Business and Community Involvement: Aligning Corporate Performance with Community Economic Development To Achieve Win:Win Impacts, Boston, Center for Corporate Community Involvement at Boston College, 2001.

> This study involves an examination of the linkages between nonprofit organizations in the community development field and corporations.

Community Relations Index, Boston, Center for Corporate Citizenship at Boston College, www.bc.edu/bc_org.
See the Center's profile of professional practices and trends in the field of community relations. The Center with 350 corporate members, publishes the CR Index, which analyzes responses to annual surveys of its members.

Community Relations Index, Boston, Center for Corporate Community Relations at Boston College, 2001.
This annual volume is based on a survey of corporate managements in the Center's membership. It provides invaluable base-line data about how the field is changing over time and how it sees its management challenges.

Corporate Community Involvement: An Annotated Bibliography: 1980-1986, Alexandria, United Way of America, 1988.
This is an excellent, 100-page integration of the early literature on strategic corporate giving. It has not been equaled by subsequent bibliographies, although the literature has mushroomed.

Corporate Philanthropy at the Crossroads, edited by Dwight Burlingame and Dennis Young, Indianapolis, Indiana University Press, 1996.
The series of essays defines a research agenda in corporate philanthropy, emphasizing the need for methodologies that measure the impact of corporate giving on corporate performance.

Corporate Social Investing: The Breakthrough Strategy for Giving and Getting Corporate Contributions, by Curt Weeden, Berrett-Kohler, 1999.
Weeden, a former director of corporate giving at Johnson & Johnson, provides a framework for how to get traction in corporate management on behalf of a corporate philanthropy program.

The Expanding Parameters of Global Corporate Citizenship, by T. Kulik, New York, Conference Board, 1999.
The report examines case studies of international corporations based in several countries to postulate the relationship between corporate citizenship and brand management and shareholder management.

"The Future of Corporate Giving," by Dwight F. Burlingame and Craig Smith, in *Serving the Public Trust: Insights into Fundraising Research and Practice,* Volume I, Paul Pribbenow, Editor, *New Directions for Philahthropic Fundraising,* Jossey-Bass Publishers, Winter, 1999, pp. 59-84.
>An overview of the various structures for corporate giving and their prospect.

Give and Take: A Candid Account of Corporate Philanthropy, by Reynold Levy, Harvard Business School Press, 1999.
>This book is a reflection of the experience of the former president of the AT&T Foundation, who helped to invent the practice of strategic corporate citizenship during his tenure.

Giving by Industry: A Reference Guide to the New Corporate Philanthropy, by Craig Smith, Washington DC, Aspen Publishers, 1999.
>In the chapter on high-tech industries, the author explains that, as companies redefined their strategies in conformity with the Internet, they re-engineered their donations programs to showcase the beneficial social uses of their technology, particularly in the field of education.

"How to Give Away Money Intelligently," by Richard Morris and Daniel Biederman, *Harvard Business Review,* 63 No. 6, November/December, 1985.
>This was the first article in a major business publication that focused on strategic corporate philanthropy. It argued that the role of the corporate giving professional is to establish charitable goals that complement business goals.

Leading Corporate Citizens: Vision, Values and Value-Added, by Sandra Waddock. New York, McGraw-Hill, 2001.
>Waddock argues that companies can find a socially beneficial path to business success by aligning their stakeholders' interests.

"The Link Between Corporate Citizenship and Financial Performance," by Stephen Garone, New York, The Conference Board, 1999.
>Unlike similar studies that argue that the best performing companies are those that emphasize corporate citizenship, this study looks for a correlation between companies that perform well financially and those that emphasize

contributions to society, and then he insists that the link exists in some instances and not others. Instead he claims that "there is no harm to shareholder value" to those companies that emphasize corporate citizenship.

Measurement De-mystified: Determining the Value of Corporate Community Involvement, Boston, Center for Corporate Citizenship at Boston College, 2001.
   The Boston College center teamed with the Productivity and Quality Center to consider options for measuring the value of corporate citizenship as a way of defending the value of the companies' support of nonprofit organizations.

"The New Corporate Philanthropy," by Craig Smith, Boston, *Harvard Business Review*, May-June, 1994.
   The article presents the paradigm of strategic corporate citizenship of new economy companies, emphasizing the case study of AT&T.

"Philanthropy and the Digital Revolution," by Craig Smith, in *The Impact of Technology on Fundraising*, Dwight F. Burlingame and Michael J. Poston, Editors, *New Directions for Philanthropic Fundraising*, Fall, 1999, pp. 59-84.
   Discusses high-tech initiatives that leverage the Internet, allowing nonprofits to reinvent themselves as prime movers for solutions to such intractable social problems as world poverty.

"Philanthropy and the Digital Revolution," by Craig Smith, in *The Impact of Technology on Fundraising*, edited by Dwight Burlingame and Michael Poston, *New Directions for Philanthropic Fundraising*, Number 25, Fall, 1999.
   In this essay, Smith argues for the strategic value of corporate/nonprofit relationships in the era of networked communications. Other articles in the issue suggest a framework for how nonprofits can build their capacities as users of technology.

Power and Influence: Mastering the Art of Persuasion, by Robert Dilenschneider, Prentice-Hall Press, New York, 1990.
   Though quite dated, the article is a classic discussion about how corporations call upon philanthropy to enhance the reputation of their brands.

"The Promotion of Corporate Citizenship," by Craig Smith, *Essays on Philanthropy*, No. 26, Center on Philanthropy at Indiana University, 1997.

> The article suggests that, in the old economy, corporate philanthropy's growth was based on advocacy. In the new economy, management considerations have replaced advocacy. A new set of measurement tools must replace the advocacy of yesterday in order to justify budgetary support for corporate philanthropy.

6. High-Tech Marketing and the Public Interest

Since the late 1980s, companies have devised a number of management techniques linking their philanthropy with their marketing. These go by various names: "cause-related marketing," "affinity marketing," "public service advertising," "community sponsorships," and "community marketing." These are sometimes confused with the term "social marketing," which refers to the way in which causes are marketed. While most social marketing is practiced by governmental and nonprofit organizations, some companies that see themselves as promoting causes as their core objective also claim to be practicing social marketing. As marketing practices have come to be transformed by e-commerce, some research is now emerging on the link between socially sensitive marketing and "e-marketing."

"Cause-Related Marketing: Case To Not Leave Home Without It," *Fund Raising Management*, 16, No. 1, March 1985.

> This is among the first writings about cause marketing, a concept invented by American Express in its support for the Statue of Liberty/Ellis Island restoration in the early 1980s. In the digital era, cause marketing has greatly expanded into forms of on-line affinity marketing.

Doing Well by Doing Good: The Marketing Link Between Business and Nonprofit Causes, by L. Lawrence Embley, Prentice-Hall, Englewood Cliffs, NJ, 1992.

> Emley argues that in the new economy, success in sales requires identifying and serving the values of customers,

which can be achieved through partnerships between corporate marketing and nonprofit organizations.

The Future of the Electronic Marketplace, by Derek Leebaert, Cambridge, MA, MIT Press, 1998.

> This collection of articles established a framework for how corporate marketing practices may change as networked communications infrastructures become more commonplace. Several authors express the point of view that this new digital marketplace can customize products and services for individual needs while still serving millions or even billions of consumers. This thesis was incorporated into high-tech signature initiatives, described in this report.

The Virtual Community: Homesteading on the Electronic Frontier, by Howard Rheingold, New York, HarperPerennial, 1994.

> This book quickly became a classic text on community building over the Internet. It seeks to define issues and challenges involved in creating online communities. Viewed from the lens of corporate management, it helped marketers to shape business strategies that emphasized the importance of building customer loyalty as a prelude to sales.

7. High-Tech R&D and the Public Interest

A small body of literature has emerged on the specific challenges to research laboratories in the high-tech sector. Few of these studies have addressed the social impact of the technologies being researched. However, the academic laboratories that have partnerships with corporations have many studies that look at "appropriate technologies" for the poor. Some of the studies note that, increasingly, R&D labs are turning to community-based settings to sponsor experimentations to close the digital divide.

"From Space Change to Real Change," by Rosabeth Moss Kanter, Boston, *Harvard Business Review*, May-June, 1999.

> The author contributes to the evolving literature on strategic corporate citizenship by arguing that, in the new digital economy, a company's nonprofit relationships can be an important source of innovations and a complement to in-house R&D activity.

Engines of Tomorrow: How the World's Best Companies Are Using Their Research Labs To Win the Future, by Robert Buderi, Simon & Schuster, New York, 2000.

Buderi examines the way high-tech corporations manage innovation and explains how the management of research helps to determine the success of companies in the new digital economy. The author in insightful in explaining how high-tech companies have sought to eliminate the walls between research and commercialization that still exist in old-economy companies. He also explains the trend towards research partnerships in which corporate research labs widen their reliance on academic and other nonprofit institutions to support their product development.

Investing in Innovation, edited by Lewis Branscomb and James Heller, Cambridge, MA, MIT Press, 1998.

This series of articles reveals the changing dynamics between federal and corporate R&D in digital technologies. It underscores the reality that the digital revolution has forced a fundamental shift in approaches to R&D by both public and private sectors.

"Out of the Laboratories and into the Developing World," by Geoffrey Kirkman, *Journal of Social Development,* 2000.

The author, a researcher at Harvard's Center for International Development, explains the trends in R&D research that cause academic and corporate laboratories to invent appropriate technologies in community-based settings in developing countries.

The Social Life of Information by John Seely Brown and Paul Duguid, Boston, Harvard Business School Press, 2000.

Written by the chief scientist at Xerox Corporation (and director of its Palo Alto Research Center, PARC), the book criticizes the mentality of technology laboratories that view the use of technologies narrowly and end up producing products that fail to serve enduring purposes. Brown argues for R&D that is drawn from an examination of human needs and processes and the social networks that people create.

Technology and the Wealth of Nations, edited by Nathan Rosenberg, Ralph London, and David Mowery, Palo Alto, Stanford University Press, 2002.

> While the title suggests that the book is a social theory about the impact of technology on economic growth, this excellent series of essays focuses on the management of innovation and suggests how new-technology companies can capture financial gain through their product-development in the digital context.

8. High-Tech Human Resources Management and the Public Interest

A growing body of literature exists on the link between volunteerism and employee morale, recruitment, retention, and productivity. Some of these studies offer case studies from high-tech corporations. In some cases, the studies point to the larger societal challenge of corporate human resources directors in increasing the numbers of technologically literate members of the work force.

"Corporate Philanthropy and Business Performance," by David Lewin and Jack Sabater, in *Corporate Philanthropy at the Crossroads*, edited by Dwight Burlingame and Dennis Young, Indiana University Press, 1996.

> A comprehensive survey of major companies indicates that companies that align their giving with employee moral-building efforts have better financial success than those that do not.

Corporate Volunteerism, Boston, Center for Corporate Community Relations at Boston College, 1999.

> The publication offers case studies of well-managed corporate volunteerism programs, including those from the high-tech sector.

Investing in Diversity: Advancing Opportunities for Minorities and the Media, Washington, DC, Aspen Institute, 1998.

> The thesis of several articles in this volume: As Internet-based corporations transform themselves into computer products companies selling their goods and services over the Internet, they will come to rely increasingly on an ethnically diverse workforce. The reasoning, in part, is that their success in e-

commerce will depend on their ability to hire and empower
ethnic minorities who can help them win the loyalty of ethnic
consumers.

"Using Technology To Strengthen Employee and Family Involvement,"
by Susan Ottenbourg, New York, The Conference Board, 1999.
This report examines how technology enters the family-support
and employee-support programs of corporations. It also looks
at corporate support for technology-based school reform.

Worker Volunteering, by Kerry Kenn Allen, New York, American
Management Association, 1980.
This is an overview of classic employee volunteerism
programs, their aspects and brief case studies of those
considered most successful at motivating volunteers.

9. High-Tech Corporate Government Affairs and the Public Interest

Not a lot of research documents the link between government
affairs strategies and philanthropy. However, a few of the studies
point out that high-tech industries have greatly increased their
investments in government relations. Further, they maintain that
the "instruments" used to advance the goals of government
relations are now more complex. In addition to conventional
"beltway" lobbying, they include media-oriented initiatives that
typically emphasize the social value of the company.

*Commanding Heights: The Battle Between Government and the
Marketplace That Is Remaking the Modern World*, by Daniel Yergin
and Joseph Stanislaw, New York, Simon and Schuster, 1998.
The authors examine the evolution of events that led to
deregulation, privatization, and other expressions of the
transfer of power from government to private hands. Further,
he considers the options for a possible reversal of these trends
by a backlash against globalization. He touches only briefly
on how information technology is reinforcing these trends
and emphasizes the implications of the integration of finance,
driven by information technology.

E-Gov: E-business Strategies for Government, by Douglas Holmes,
London, Brealy Publishing, 2001.

The author looks beyond automation of government offices to applications of digital technology that transform the functioning of governments.

"Information Age Impacts on Governance: Could This Be the Start of Something Big?" by Jerry Mechling, August, 1998. unpublished manuscript.

The article, written by a Harvard Kennedy School expert on governance, explains the challenges of how government bureaus are seeking to reinvent themselves with the help of technology and how high-tech corporations are contributing to that effort through their government-relations divisions.

Redefining Corporate-Federal Relations, Phyllis McGrath, New York, The Conference Board, 1997.

This report provides case studies that show how high-tech (and other) corporations no longer isolate their federal relations in Washington offices but work through media, nonprofits, and their own employees to advance their goals in government relations.

Six Degrees of Competition: Correlating Regulation with the Telecommunications Marketplace, by Robert Entman and Michael Katz, Washington, DC, Aspen Institute, 2000.

A report for an Aspen roundtable, this report argues for realigning telecommunications regulation to the realities of the marketplace in the digital economy.

Towards an Information Bill of Rights and Responsibilities, edited by Charles Firestone, Washington DC, Aspen Institute, 1995.

The series of essays looks beyond the existing framework to offer proposals for regulating high-tech and media corporations.

Unchartered Territory: New Frontiers of Digital Innovation, by David Bollier, Washington, Aspen Institute, 2001.

The result of an Aspen roundtable, this report seeks to define the public policy challenges in the new economy and sets out a framework for a new antitrust policy aimed at fostering innovation and reducing inequities.

Index

3Com   9, 10, 18, 58, 90

A —
Acer   10, 89, 108
Adobe   10
advertising   36-41, 45, 124
affinity marketing   36, 40-42, 124
Allen, Paul   11
Akers, John   23, 24, 38
Amazon.com   10, 40-42
American Association of Community Colleges   33, 58
American Library Association   18, 33
Ameritech   10, 96
Annan, Kofi   8
anti-globalization   13, 74, 89, 95
antipoverty   5, 97
AOL Time Warner   9-10, 19, 46, 53, 63, 99, 104
Apple   10, 17, 30, 44, 53
Applied Materials   24
Armstrong, Arthur G.   41
AT&T   10, 15-17, 28-29, 43, 53, 56, 61, 90, 98, 122-123
AT&T Language Line   43

B —
Bangalore   10, 67, 87
Bay Networks   10
Bell Atlantic   10, 28, 82
Bell South   10, 20, 28
Benton Foundation   11, 46, 92
Berresford, Susan   7
Bertelsmann   10, 18
Bezos, Jeff   11, 40
Bill & Melinda Gates Foundation   34, 104
business practice   3, 6, 9, 12, 35

C —
Case, Steve   24, 99, 104
Center for Technology and Society   32
certification programs   5, 22, 45, 58, 101

Hewlett-Packard   5, 6, 10, 30, 37, 47, 54, 56, 62, 76, 118
high-tech corporations   1, 3, 7, 8, 13, 27, 61-62, 90, 114, 128, 129
human resources   25, 51, 107, 127

I —

IBM   17, 29-30, 38, 48, 53, 56, 58, 60-61, 82-83
InfoSpace   10
InfoSys   9, 10, 67
Intel   10, 17, 20, 55
intellectual transfer   36

J —

Joint Venture: Silicon Valley   11, 24, 69

K —

K-12 education   18, 26, 69
Kellogg Foundation   8, 11
Knowledge Universe   10, 44

L —

Lotus Development Corporation   10, 53
Lucent Technologies   10, 16, 20, 93

M —

market development   18, 36, 39
marketing unit   2, 16, 27
Markle Foundation   8, 11, 43
McCaw, Craig   11
MCI   10, 15, 18, 25, 28, 29, 90
Microland   10
Microsoft   6, 7, 10, 18, 20, 31, 32, 33, 34, 37, 44, 45, 51, 56, 63,
     69, 72, 74, 78, 81, 82, 90, 104
middle management   2, 12, 119
MIT Media Lab   9, 11, 48, 83, 85, 86, 87
Morgan, Becky   24
Motorola   10, 35, 37, 47, 85, 102, 103

N —

NEC   10
Netscape   10
New York City   9, 73, 90, 93
Nokia   10, 37
Northern Telecom   10, 56
Novel   10, 18

O —

Open Society Institute   8, 21
Oracle   10, 17, 18, 45, 57, 58, 64, 65, 78, 104

P —
Pacific Bell   10, 95, 96
Pacific Century CyberWorks   9, 10
partnerships   7, 24, 37, 39, 48, 69, 101-102, 114, 115
product giveaways   36, 42

Q —
Quest   10

R —
RealNetworks   9-10, 56, 105
Rockefeller Foundation   8

S —
Sabatar, Jack   29
San Francisco   9, 24, 55, 96
SBC Communications   10, 17, 95
Schwab, Charles   11
Seattle   9, 11, 31, 32, 34, 42, 47, 56, 69, 89
senior management   15, 25, 89
Siemens   10
signature initiative   1, 2, 12-13, 15-18, 20, 25, 27, 30, 72, 104, 118
Silicon Graphics   10, 34
Silicon Valley   24, 34, 55, 58, 66, 67, 74, 103
Silverman, Fred   30
Skoll, Jeff 34
Softbank   10
Sony   10, 37
Sprint   10, 57, 90
Stonesifer, Patty   34
Strahn, Diane   10, 15, 24, 28
strategic corporate philanthropy   12, 27-28, 35, 122
Sun Microsystems   10, 34, 69, 74, 90, 113

T —
Telenor   10, 12, 105
Telstra   10
Thompson, Samme   35, 102

U —
United Communications   10
United Nations   7, 8, 11, 22, 73, 85, 89, 99, 115, 116
United Negro College Fund   45, 56

V —
Viacom   10

W —
WorldCom   10, 15, 16, 24, 29, 53, 72, 74
World e-Inclusion   5,6 76-77, 118